Be Expert with
Map and Compass

The "ORIENTEERING" Handbook

NEW REVISED EDITION

D0958741

BE EXPERT WITH
MAP AND COMPASS

THE "ORIENTEERING"® HANDBOOK

(NEW-Revised edition)

By

Bjorn Kjellstrom

Illustrated by
Francis J. Rigney

Maps by
U. S. Geological Survey

CHARLES SCRIBNER'S SONS
NEW YORK

Copyright 1955, © 1967 Bjorn Kjellstrom

All rights reserved. No part of this book
may be reproduced in any form without the
permission of Charles Scribner's Sons.

A–10.72(V)

Printed in the United States of America
Library of Congress Catalog Card Number 72-7879
SBN 684-13091-2

TABLE OF CONTENTS

Orienteering ®

Finding your way — Finding yourself

Science, mathematics — And the divine thing called LOVE:

Love of NATURE.

Intense exertion — Explorers' pride

Wholesome solitude — And glorious comradeship!

ORIENTEERING is a coined word, registered in the U.S.A. and Canada for services rendered and products distributed by American Orienteering Service, La Porte, Indiana, and by Canadian Orienteering Services, Toronto, Ont. Canada.

FOREWORD

This book is written for two purposes mainly:

First of all, to give YOU, personally, a chance to join in the fun which is being experienced by an ever-increasing number of outdoorsmen (and women) through an imaginative use of map and compass in finding your own way and being your own guide, whether along highways or through the wilderness.

And, secondly, to attempt to make you so enthusiastic about the potentialities of map-and-compass-work in the form of "Orienteering" that you will want to help OTHERS share your enjoyment.

To achieve these purposes, every effort has been made to present the necessary map-and-compass theories as painlessly as possible—not just for your own edification, but also for simplifying the job of teaching the theories to others. And to help you in mastering the skills involved, a large number of specific practices have been included, suitable for self-testing and for group games and projects.

Skill with map and compass cannot be learned from book reading only. They must be learned through practice—through the actual handling and using of the tools of Orienteering, map and compass, in combination with a steadily developing power of observation. To get your practice under way as quickly as possible, this book is provided with a training map, a training compass, and a practicing protractor. The use of these items from the very beginning in conjunction with your reading should move you quickly into the world of mastering map and compass in your newfound experience with ORIENTEERING.

This Handbook of Orienteering is the result of many years of personal experience in this fascinating field, including active participation and instruction in competitive Orienteering racing on an international level. The book deals primarily with instruction in map-and-compass work according to modern methods, with suggestions for practice games appropriate to each step in learning. The text is addressed to the outdoorsman in general but is also meant to promote among younger readers an interest in Orienteering as a sport. Those readers who might become interested in competitive

Orienteering racing (cross-country running with map and compass) will find some basic information in a special chapter. For the finer details and techniques used in competitive Orienteering racing I refer to textbooks now available.

I owe a large measure of thanks to a great number of organizations and individuals. They have contributed in various ways, directly or indirectly, by providing ideas and by fostering an enthusiasm for the sport of Orienteering. Among organizations the following should be specifically mentioned: American Association for Health, Physical Education and Recreation; National Recreation Association; American Camping Association; Boy Scouts International Bureau; Boy Scouts of America; Canadian Boy Scouts Association; Girl Scouts of the U.S.A.; Canadian Girl Guides Association; The International Orienteering Federation; The United States Orienteering Federation and The Canadian Orienteering Federation. Also such agencies as the Map Information Office of the Geological Survey, U.S. Department of the Interior; Department of Education, Ontario, Canada; Department of National Health and Welfare, Physical Fitness Division, Ottawa, Canada; the U.S. Army Infantry School and the Physical Fitness Academy of the U.S. Marine Corps.

Many individuals have also shared in the writing of this volume. They are simply too many to be mentioned here. I do owe special thanks, however, to William Hillcourt, "Green Bar Bill" of the Boy Scouts of America and *Boys' Life* magazine and well-known writer on outdoor life, who contributed a great deal by editing the text.

To him and to all supporters and helpers my sincere thanks!

And now — may you, the reader, by studying this book and by following its suggestions, lay a foundation for an interest in outdoor life and Orienteering which will remain with you always. Have fun!

BJORN KJELLSTROM

Introducing:

THE ART OF ORIENTEERING

With every passing year, America is getting more and more outdoor-conscious. Her roads are teeming with cars, her parks with visitors, her outdoor trails with hikers and campers.

Most of the travelers go by route numbers or trail signs. But an increasing number of them strike out by themselves along little-known paths, or cross-country.

Whichever way you travel—whether you follow the main lanes of our country or its byways—you will get far more fun out of your experience if you are thoroughly familiar with the use of map and compass.

"But why bother with map and compass," you may say, "when the roads are numbered, the trails clearly marked?"

Because map reading today is an essential part of any person's basic knowledge—whether for traveling or for keeping track of events in our own country and around the world.

Because the ability to use a compass in the field is an outdoor skill that will help to make you self-reliant and confident in all your travelings.

Because the use of map and compass together opens up chances for greater enjoyment of traveling and of the out-of-doors than you have ever experienced before.

With map and compass for your steady companions, the art of *Orienteering*—the skill of finding your way along highways and country roads, through woods and fields, through mountain territory and over lakes—becomes an intriguing hobby and an interesting sport, whether you travel alone or with a buddy or with a group of like-minded friends.

Map and Compass in Your Everyday Life

Fundamentally, we all make use of maps and compass directions in our everyday lives—consciously or unconsciously.

When you sit down to plan a trip—whether by automobile, rail, ship, air, or on foot—you get out maps or charts and try to figure out the shortest way, or the best way, or the route that will take you past the greatest number of interesting places. Then, on the trip, you consult your maps repeatedly to check where you are and where you are to go.

When someone asks you for directions in town or country, or when someone gives them to you, your brain automatically attempts to draw a small map of the location. In your mind, you see the roads as lines, the rivers as bands, the buildings as small squares—exactly the way they are represented on a map.

Map and Compass for the Outdoorsman

If you are a hunter or a fisherman, you will have done much of your traveling to your favorite hunting spot or trout stream by map and compass—unless you have depended on a guide. In territory you know well from having traversed it again and again, the lay of the land and the different directions will be part of your working memory. When it comes to new territory, on the other hand, you have probably pored over maps and compass, and have used them in the field to find your way to the best hunting ground, the best-stocked lake.

The experienced outdoorsman has no fear or uncertainty about traveling through strange territory—map and compass will get him there and safely back again.

Foresters, surveyors, engineers, prospectors, men in the armed services all require thorough training in Orienteering with map and compass. The yachtsman needs a sound knowledge of map or chart and compass to navigate our waterways.

And if you happen to be a leader of Boy Scouts or Explorers, of Girl Scouts or Camp Fire Girls, or a camp counselor taking your campers on a cross-country hike, or a teacher with your pupils on a field trip, you will readily recognize the need to know the proper use of map and compass so that you may transmit that knowledge to the boys or girls in your charge, and help them to get along safely and securely in the outdoors. In addition, you will know that map study and compass use can be translated into a great number of interesting games and projects and competitions for meeting room, club room or class room, and for hike trail and camp site.

And if you are none of these, but simply a vacationer in a State or a National Park, or a Sunday stroller in the woods, you will still discover

The early pioneer scout knew how to find his way through the wilderness. His "pathfinding" skill is kept alive by the modern orienteerer.

that a map and a compass will increase the fun of your vacationing or your hiking.

The Romance of Orienteering

But besides the added enjoyment, there is a real satisfaction in mastering the art of using map and compass.

There has always been a romantic fascination to persons who could find their way through the wilderness and over hidden trails — the Indian, the pioneer scout, the guide, the tracker, the explorer. There seemed to be a mysterious power behind their remarkable capacity for pathfinding.

In the old days, this pathfinding was well-worth admiration. It was based on a highly developed power of observation and of remembering — reading the signs of mountain ridges and rivers and vegetation, wind directions and cloud movements, the position of sun and moon and stars.

Today, pathfinding is a much simpler matter with a good map and a dependable, modern compass.

Where the old-timer learned his skill the hard way over a great number of years, the outdoorsmen of today can learn the secrets of Orienteering in a matter of hours.

And when you have mastered the skill, it sticks!

It will help you on all your outdoor expeditions. It will make you feel safe and certain in the wildest territory. It will make it possible for you to cut down travel distance and travel time through shortcuts. It will challenge you to explore out-of-the-way places of special interest. It will show you the way to new camp sites and fishing lakes and hunting grounds.

And, eventually, it may turn you into a protagonist for ORIENTEERING as a sport — helping others to enjoy themselves in exciting cross-country traveling.

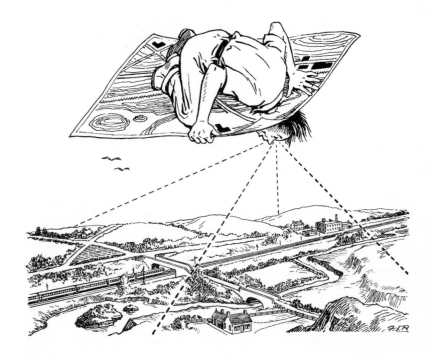

PART I

FUN WITH MAPS ALONE

There is a tale in the Arabian Nights' Entertainment of a magnificent contraption: A magic carpet. The lucky owner could seat himself on his carpet, recite the proper magic formula—and suddenly the carpet would rise in the air and carry him wherever he wanted to go.

Imagine yourself traveling cross-country on that kind of a carpet—or on its modern equivalent, an airplane. It is a bright day—visibility unlimited. The sky above is blue. Below, the ground spreads before you in a multi-colored crazy quilt pattern. First everything is just a jumble of details. But soon certain things begin to stand out.

That straight ribbon down there, for example, must be the highway —Route 66, or whatever it happens to be. Now it crosses a wide, winding band—obviously a river. You can even make out the bridge as two short lines—the bridge railings. The rectangles down there are house tops, the dark-green masses surely forests. Things look different from what you are accustomed to—yet you recognize them in their reduced dimensions.

WHAT A MAP IS

If you took a camera shot of what you see below, and later printed it up in a fair size, you would have a photographic "map" of the area over which you flew—with a lot of confusing details, and with distortions toward the edges because of perspective, but a "map" nevertheless: *a reduced representation of a portion of the surface of the earth.*

The modern map maker uses aerial photographs in his map making and checks them through surveys in the field. But in the final map, he simplifies details into simple, representative signs—he calls them "map symbols"—and flattens out the perspective so that every small section of the map looks the way it would appear to you flying directly over it and looking straight down on it, and so that all distances are in the same proportion on the map as they are in the landscape.

What Kind of Map to Get

Maps are made for numerous different purposes: State highway maps for automobiling, city maps for the use of city departments—fire, sanitation, and others—nautical charts for sea travel, and many more. Few of these would be of much help to you in Orienteering.

Topographic Maps

The kind of map that will serve you best is called a "topographic" map —from the Greek *topos,* place, and *graphein,* to write or draw: a drawing or a picture of a place or an area.

Such topographic maps are available for large areas of the United States and of Canada. In the United States, they are prepared by the U. S. Geological Survey of the Department of the Interior; in Canada, by the Surveys and Mapping Branch of the Department of Mines and Technical Surveys.

What Scale to Pick

Each topographic map is drawn to a specific scale. Such a scale is the proportion between a distance on the map and the actual distance in the

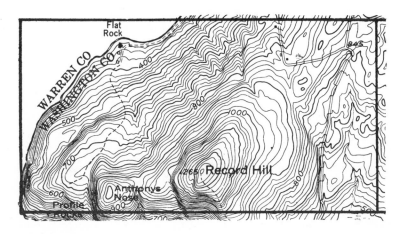

1:24,000 maps are best suited for orienteering because of the great number of details they contain. Compare this map with maps on pages 8 and 9.

field, or, stated in another way: The amount that a distance in the field has been reduced for inclusion on the map.

For the sake of simplicity, these map scales have been developed in such a way that it is easy to measure map distances with the measurements with which you are already familiar: The inches and fractions of inches of an ordinary ruler. One unit measured on the map means so many units in the field, one inch so many inches.

The three scales most commonly used are the scales of 1 unit to 24,000 units, 1 unit to 62,500 units, and 1 unit to 250,000 units.

On the map, these proportionate scales are indicated by a fraction:

$$1:24,000 \text{ or } \frac{1}{24,000}, \ 1:62,500 \text{ or } \frac{1}{62,500}, \text{ and } 1:250,000 \text{ or } \frac{1}{250,000}.$$

The larger the fraction (the fraction 1 divided by 24,000 is obviously larger than 1 divided by 250,000), the larger and clearer the details shown on it. But on the other hand, the larger the fraction, the smaller the territory covered by the same size map sheet.

But why these specific fractions? The reason is simple — and suggests the map scale best suited to your needs:

1:24,000 Maps — If you pick the inch for your measuring unit, 1 inch to 24,000 inches means that a distance of 1 inch on your map is

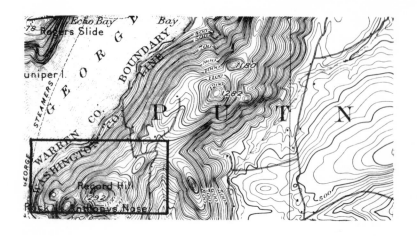

1:62,500 maps are helpful in giving you a general idea of the lay of the land in your area. Compare rectangle at left with map on page 7.

24,000 inches in the field. That number of inches translated into feet becomes 2,000 feet—a measurement easily used in surveying.

Maps on a scale of 1:24,000 are made of areas of general public interest. They cover an area ranging from 49 square miles (along the Canadian border), to 68 square miles (in southern Texas and Florida).

For finding your way in a limited area within a radius of, say, 4 miles, and for general orienteering practices, the map of a scale of 1:24,000 would be your choice.

(For certain sections of the country, a scale of 1:31,680 has been used in the preparation of large-scale maps. This scale is being continued only in a few localities where the status of previously published maps or other local circumstances make the use of the 1:24,000 scale inadvisable for the time being.)

1:62,500 Maps—The scale of 1 inch to 62,500 inches may seem cumbersome, until it is realized that 1 inch on the map to that many inches in the field means almost exactly 1 inch on the map to 1 mile in the field. To be completely correct, the scale should really be 1:63,360, since there are 63,360 inches to the mile—but 62,500 is close enough for most purposes, and certainly simpler in surveying. Also, this scale is an easy multiple of the 1:250,000 scale.

Maps on a scale of 1:62,500 are available of areas of average public

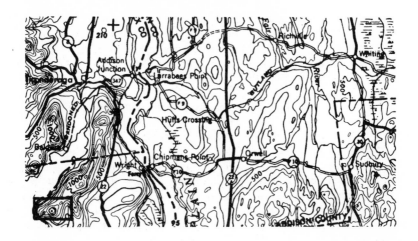

1:250,000 maps will assist you in finding new places to explore. Compare small rectangle at left with the maps on pages 7 and 8.

interest. Each map covers an area that ranges from 195 square miles in the northern part of our country to 271 square miles in the southern states. It is one of the objectives of the Geological Survey ultimately to publish maps at this scale of the entire area of the continental United States.

A map of your locality on the scale of 1:62,500 would be particularly helpful to you if you intend to cover your area intensively, or to go in for more advanced Orienteering.

1:250,000 Maps — The scale of 1 inch to 250,000 inches is almost exactly the scale of 1 inch to 4 miles. The correct figure would be 253,440 — a number which would obviously require a lot of unnecessary work in surveying.

Maps on the scale of 1:250,000 are now in the process of preparation and publication by the U. S. Geological Survey. These maps cover an area of 6,346 to 8,668 square miles.

A map on the scale of 1:250,000 will give you a general idea of the geographic features of your region. It will assist you in discovering points of interest within a distance of 100 miles, and will prove valuable in planning trips and expeditions.

Where to Get Topographic Maps

United States Maps — You get your topographic maps through the U. S. Geological Survey — in these two steps:

1. Your first step for getting a map of an area in the United States is to drop a postcard to:

> *Map Information Office,*
> *United States Geological Survey,*
> *Washington, D. C. 20242*

(you will find such a postcard, ready for mailing, in the envelope in the back of this book) and request a *Topographic Map Index Circular* of the State in which your area is located, and the Geological Survey booklet on *Topographic Maps.* This material is free.

The Index Circular contains a map of the whole State, divided into rectangles — "quadrangles." Each quadrangle map covers à certain area and is designated by the name of a town or some natural feature within the area.

2. Study the Index Circular and decide what maps you need. Then send in your order, specifying "woodland" copies, and remitting by money order or check 50 cents for each map (except for 1:250,000 maps which are 75 cents each).

For maps of areas EAST of the Mississippi River send your order to

> *Distribution Section,*
> *Geological Survey,*
> *Washington, D. C. 20242*

For maps of areas WEST of the Mississippi River send your order to

> *Distribution Section,*
> *Geological Survey,*
> *Denver Federal Center,*
> *Denver, Colorado. 80225*

Canadian Maps — For maps of areas in Canada, write to the Map Distribution Office, Department of Mines and Technical Surveys, Ottawa, Ontario, Canada.

Other Maps — For areas not covered by regular topographic maps, there are many other maps available — such as U. S. Forest Service maps (obtainable from U. S. Forest Service, Washington, D. C. 20250), or National Parks maps (for information write to U. S. National Park Service, Washington, D. C. 20252). Your local Chamber of Commerce or Surveying Office, or your State's Department of Conservation may also have valuable information or suggestions.

WHAT THE MAP TELLS

The map is the outdoorsman's "reader." If you know how, you can read a map as easily as you can read a book. It will tell you what you want to know about the geographical features of the area in which you intend to travel. It does this under five categories—the five D's of map reading:

To know what is meant by these five headings, unroll the topographic map you ordered, spread it out flat, and take a good look at it.

Your map didn't arrive yet? Well, don't let that delay your map study. In that case, open up the training map in the back of the book and use that. This map is about one-third of the map surface of an actual U. S. Geological Survey topographic quadrangle map on the scale of 1:24,000 —part of map number N4345-W7322.5/7.5, to be exact. In printing this map section for this book, the margin was trimmed, but the descriptive matter of the margin was retained; it is inserted in the text that follows in such a way that you will know exactly to which item the text refers.

Description

The description of the map is found in its margin. So let's take a trip the whole way around the margin of a representative topographic map and read all the information that is pertinent to the use of that map.

Name of Map Area

The type material at the right top margin contains the name of the main feature on the map—a town, a lake, a mountain, or some other prominent location. That is the quadrangle name you used in ordering the map.

This name is repeated at the bottom right, with the number of the map.

In small type at top and bottom, at each side, and at each corner, are the names of the quadrangles that border on your map. Those are the names you'll use if you want to order maps of the neighboring areas.

Location

Your map is a reduced section of some spot of our globe. But where on that great sphere? Your map tells you.

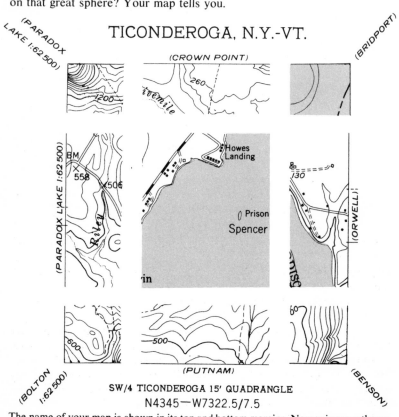

The name of your map is shown in its top and bottom margins. Names in parentheses give you the designations of the neighboring maps.

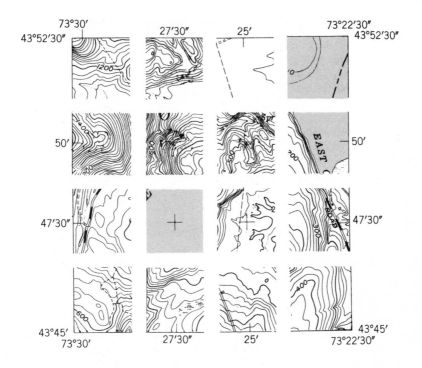

Numbers at top and bottom are longitude degrees, numbers at sides latitude degrees. Note cross-marks where connecting lines intersect.

Directly over the top line that frames the map area, and under the bottom line of it, are some small numerals, and tiny lines jut into the map from them. At each side of the map are similar numbers, and similar tiny lines.

With the help of those numbers and lines you can find the exact place on the globe where your area is located.

If you connect the tiny lines at the top of the map with the corresponding lines at the bottom, you are drawing *meridian lines* that run true north to true south—lines which, elongated far enough, would hit the North Pole in one direction, the South Pole in the other. The numbers attached to these lines are degrees of longitude, figured westward from the zero degree line that runs through Greenwich, England.

If you connect the tiny lines at one side of the map with the corresponding lines at the other, you are drawing *parallel lines*—lines that

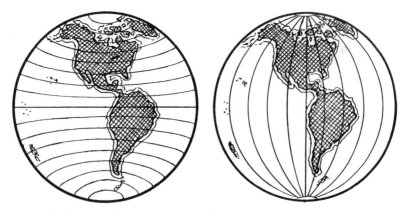

Longitude lines run from pole to pole, latitude lines around globe. Zero longitude is at Greenwich, England; zero latitude is Equator.

run parallel to the Equator. The numbers at these lines are degrees of latitude, figured northward from Equator in the Northern Hemisphere, and southward from Equator in the Southern Hemisphere. Equator itself has the dubious honor of having the zero degree.

Longitude — latitude . . . care to remember the difference? Then think of their origin: Both of them from Latin words used by the Romans to indicate the shape of the Mediterranean Sea — the lines that cut the length of it: *longitude,* and the lines that cut the width of it: *latitude.*

Dates

Down at the bottom of the map are some dates of importance to you as a map user: To the left, for instance, the information "Aerial photographs taken 1942. Field check 1949-1950," and to the right simply "1950" (see illustration on page 44).

The map before you was developed on the basis of aerial photographs taken in the year 1942, drawn, and checked by surveyors in the field during the period 1949-1950. The edition you have was printed in 1950.

Well, a number of things may have happened in the area covered by the map since the field check in 1950: If a town is shown, it has probably grown. The road through town may have become a highway. The swamp north of the town may have been dried out, a dam may have been built across the river to form a lake.

So keep in mind that your map was correct for the year it was checked,

"Longitude" and "latitude" are from Latin words used to indicate size of Mediterranean Sea. Longitude lines give length of the Mediterranean.

and don't worry too much if a few changes have been made since then. Just take the possibility into consideration when you plan your traveling through the area.

Details — Map Symbols

To show the details of a landscape, different signs are used — *map symbols*. The map symbols are mapping's alphabet — together they spell out the lay of the land. These map symbols are not arbitrary marks. On the contrary, the people who invented them made every effort, within reason, to have the signatures look like the things they represent.

The main symbols used on topographic maps are pictured on the pages that follow. All of them are found in the Geological Survey's free folder, *Topographic Maps,* mentioned on page 10.

For orienteering purposes, you are mainly interested in four types of map symbols, each with its own distinctive color:

> *Man-made features,* or *cultural features*
> *Water features,* or *hydrographic features*
> *Vegetation features*
> *Elevation features,* or *hypsographic features*

Man-Made Features

Under the category of features made by man, we have his roads and trails, his houses and public buildings, his railroads and power lines, his

Hard surface highway, heavy duty . . . .

Hard surface highway, medium duty . . . . . red

Improved dirt road . . . .

Unimproved dirt road . . . .

Trail . . . .

Bridge, road . . . .

Footbridge . . . .

Ford, road . . . .   Ford   =Fd=

dams and bridges, the boundaries he has set between his areas. These features are shown on the map in BLACK — with the exception of heavy-duty and medium-duty highways which are sometimes overprinted with RED to distinguish them from less important roads.

Generally speaking, the symbols for man-made features show the fea-

Map Symbols for MAN-MADE FEATURES — Black

Single track railroad . . . .

Multiple main line track railroad . . . .

Buildings (barn, warehouse, etc.) . . . .

Buildings (dwelling, place of employment) .

School . . . .

Church . . . .

Cemetery . . . . [t] [Cem]

Telephone, telegraph, pipe line, etc. . . . . . .

Power transmission line . . . .

Open pit or quarry . . . .

tures much larger than they should really be. This is done for clarity. A road 20 feet wide, for instance, on a 1:24,000 scale map, should only be one one-hundred of an inch thick — obviously much too thin to be very distinct. Instead, it is shown as a double line. If your measuring on a map involves a road, use middle of road as actual point of measurement.

Map Symbols for WATER FEATURES — Blue

Lake or pond . . . .

Perennial streams . . . .

Spring . . . .

Water well . . . .

Marsh or swamp . . . .

Improved roads are shown by solid double lines; unimproved roads by dashed double lines; trails by dashed single lines.

Railroads are indicated by full lines with tiny cross-lines to suggest the railroad ties.

Water Features

On topographic maps, rivers and canals, lakes and oceans, swamps and marshes, and other bodies of water are printed in BLUE.

Brooks and narrow rivers are indicated by a single line, larger rivers by a blue band. Large bodies of water are usually shown with a light blue tint, with a shore line in darker blue.

Vegetation Features

On recent maps of the United States Geological Survey, a GREEN tint is used to indicate wooded areas, orchards, vineyards, and scrub.

For Orienteering purposes, it is important for you to know whether an area is wooded or not — therefore, when ordering your map, specify "woodland copy" just to be certain that you receive a map with this overprinting.

Map Symbols for VEGETATION FEATURES — Green

Woods — brushwood . . . . | solid green tint |

Orchard . . . .

Vineyard . . . .

Scrub . . . .

Elevation Features — Hills and Valleys

The ups and downs of an area — its mountains and hills, its valleys and plains — are shown on the topographic map by thin BROWN lines, "contour lines."

While most of the other map symbols are quite self-evident, the contour lines will probably need some explanation.

A contour line, by definition, is an imaginary line on the ground along which every point is at the same height above sea level (although, occasionally, some other reference datum is used).

Unfold the training map in the back of the book. Study those thin, brown contour lines. You will discover that every fifth line is heavier than the others. Follow one of those heavier lines and you will find a number on it. That number indicates that every point along that line is that many feet above sea level — that many feet above the average level of the nearest ocean, the Atlantic or the Pacific. Let's say that the number you have found on the contour is 500. If the Atlantic Ocean should suddenly rise 500 feet above its mean level of 0 feet and pour into the landscape, the contour line marked 500 would become the new shore line.

The distance in height between one contour line and the one next to it is called the "contour interval." What is meant by contour interval? Simply this, that if the water in our imaginary flood should rise by a certain number of feet indicated on the map, the next contour line would be the new shore line. The contour interval varies from map to map. On a great number of topographic maps the contour interval is 20 feet —among them the map of which the training map is a section. On a map of a rather level area, the contour interval may be as little as 5 feet, and on maps of mountainous territories as much as 50 feet or more— there just wouldn't be room on the map for all those 5- or even 20-foot interval lines. The contour interval of the map you secure from the Geological Survey is found in a note printed in the bottom margin—

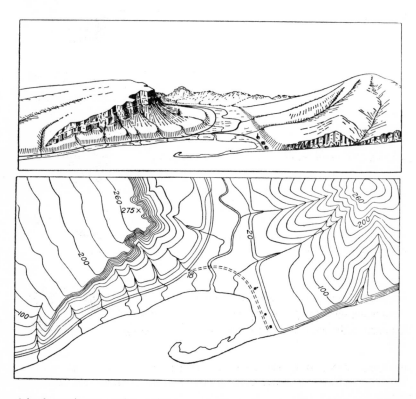

A landscape in perspective, and the same landscape in contour lines. Note especially that lines are far apart for level land, almost touch for cliffs.

Map Symbols for ELEVATION Features — Brown

Index contour .... ━━━━━━━━━━

Intermediate contour .... ──────────

Depression contours ....

Cut ....

Fill ....

Large earth dam or levee ....

Sand area, sand dunes ....

Triangulation or transit traverse station .... △
    monumented with spirit level elev. .... BM△ 1062
Monumented bench mark, spirit level elev. ...... BM× 958

such as CONTOUR INTERVAL 20 FEET — but you can figure it out for yourself by studying the numbers on the contour lines of your map.

You'll probably find the contour lines a bit confusing in the beginning, but you will soon get to look at each hill and mountain in terms of contour lines. Then, when successive contour lines are close together, they will tell you that the area is steep; when they run together they indicate a cliff; when they are far apart they show a gentle slope.

The heights of many points — such as road intersections, summits, surfaces of lakes, and benchmarks — are also given on the map in figures which show altitude to the nearest foot.

Simple demonstration of contour lines; Dip rock part-way in water, draw water line. Dip one inch deeper, draw other line. And so on. View from above.

Map Symbol Practices — Now, before you continue, test your knowledge of map symbols, to make certain that they stick in your memory. And if you are working with others, test them, too, turning the testing into interesting games or practices.

MAP SYMBOL QUIZ   INDOOR PRACTICE

PURPOSE — A quick review of the map symbols to make sure that they are mastered.

TEST YOURSELF — Study the map symbols on page 23. Then, without referring to the illustrations on the preceding pages, write the name of each symbol on the line below it. Don't peek now — but the correct names are found on page 131.

AS GAME — Copy page 23 onto a blackboard, OR cut a mimeograph stencil and run off as many copies as you have players, OR purchase

MAP SYMBOL QUIZ

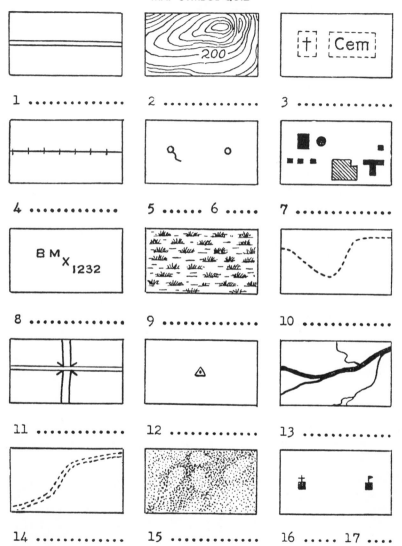

1 .... 2 .... 3 ....

4 .... 5 ...... 6 ...... 7 ....

8 .... 9 .... 10 ....

11 .... 12 .... 13 ....

14 .... 15 .... 16 ..... 17 ....

Read instructions for this Map Symbol Quiz on page 22. Objective is to write on dotted lines the names of the symbols. Used as a game, have this sheet mimeographed, or get copies from American Orienteering Service.

the necessary number of printed Map Symbol Quiz Sheets (from American Orienteering Service — see order blank in back of book). Distribute sheets to players, with a pencil to each. Give 5 minutes for filling in the names. Score 5 points for each correct name; up to 85 points for all 17 names correct.

IMAGINARY MAP SKETCHING   INDOOR PRACTICE

PURPOSE — To get a general idea of how map symbols relate to each other.

TEST YOURSELF — Study a small section of the training map in the back of the book, then get out a letterhead-size piece of paper and a pencil. Attempt to sketch, from memory, the map section you have just studied, incorporating in it as many map symbols as possible. Particularly important: how roads and rivers run in relation to each other, where buildings are located, where crossroads lead, and so on.

AS GAME — Give each player paper and pencil, then dictate slowly the lay of the land of an imaginary territory, such as: "Draw a highway from the top left corner of the paper to the bottom right corner. Place a spring at the top right corner. Start a stream from this spring and run it to the middle of the paper until it hits the road. Make a bridge on the road across the stream. Continue the stream on the other side of the bridge and have it run into a small lake at the bottom left of your paper. Place a school on the right side of the road, just above the bridge . . ." And so on, using about a dozen map symbols. When the maps are completed, have the players judge each others' maps and vote to decide which is best.

CONTOUR QUIZ   INDOOR PRACTICE

PURPOSE — To be able to read the meaning of contour lines, quickly and correctly.

TEST YOURSELF — Read the questions, then study the training map, and underline the words below which you believe most nearly describe the actual conditions. Answers on page 131 — but don't look now.

1. You are walking the road from Log Chapel to the cross-roads north of it. The road is (a) almost level, (b) uphill, (c) downhill.

2. Charter Brook runs (a) from bottom of map to top of map, (b) from top of map to bottom of map.

3. You are walking inland 400 feet on the road from Glenburnie. Your route is (a) a steep climb, rising 100 feet, (b) a slow grade, rising only 40 feet.

4. Sucker Brook is (a) a slow-moving stream, (b) a fast-moving stream.

5. When you stand on hill marked 400, about one-half mile north of Meadow Knoll Cemetery, you should be able to see (a) Hutton Hill, (b) Meadow Knoll Cemetery, (c) Niger Marsh, (d) Log Chapel, (e) Huckleberry Mountain.

AS GAME — Distribute copies of training maps (from Orienteering Training Kit, see page 133) to the participants. Then begin: "Find Log Chapel, then follow the road northward to the cross-road. Is the road almost level, or are you going uphill, or downhill? And how do you know?" First player to put up hand and answer the question correctly scores 20 points — and so on, until all five questions have been answered for a possible total of 100 points.

Directions

A quick glance at a map will show you the relative direction in which any point lies from any other point. But when you want to find the actual direction between two points, as related to the north and the south of the landscape, you need to know first of all what is north and what is south on the map as a whole.

Which Map Direction Is North?

When you place a topographic map before you with the reading matter right side up, you can be pretty certain that what's up is north and what's

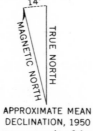

APPROXIMATE MEAN
DECLINATION, 1950

The declination diagram in the bottom margin of the map indicates the angle between the true-north and the magnetic-north direction of the map area.

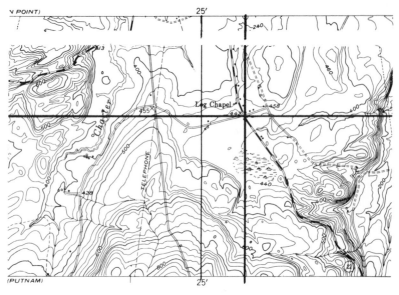

Draw longitude meridian lines, then a parallel meridian through your "base of operations." Find out what lies north and south, east and west of base.

down is south. Which means that the left margin as you look at the map is west, the right margin east.

If there is any doubt in your mind about how the directions lie on your map, look in the bottom margin. Here you will find a small diagram of an angle with one leg marked TRUE NORTH – the other leg is marked Magnetic North, but don't bother about that just now. Simply ascertain that the line marked TRUE NORTH runs parallel to the lines that frame the map on the left and on the right.

What Direction Is It?

Now spread out your topographic map in front of you – or use the training map in the back of the book. Find a longitude number along the top line of the map frame, and the corresponding number along the bottom line of the frame. With a ruler and a pencil, draw a line between the two marks at the longitude numbers. This north-south line is one of the meridian lines described on page 13.

Decide on some specific spot on this meridian line, and make that spot your "base of operations" for your practice in determining directions.

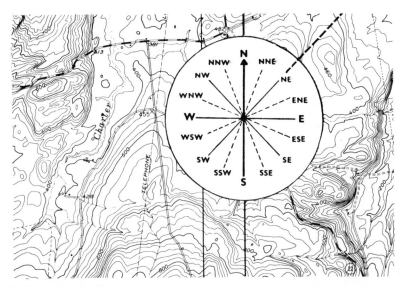

To determine what lies in other directions from your "base of operations," make use of a folded paper circle. Place center of circle over your base.

First of all, follow the meridian line from that spot up toward the top of the map from that spot—any point on the meridian line is directly north of your spot. Follow the meridian line down toward the bottom of the map from your base spot—any point on the meridian line is directly south of the spot. Go directly to the left of the spot—any point here is west of the spot. Go directly to the right of it—any point here is east of the spot.

Finding Map Directions with a Paper Circle

But what about all the other directions from your "base of operations"?

To help you determine some of those directions, take a piece of paper, about three inches square. Fold it with sharp folds in half, then in quarters, then in eighths, finally in sixteenths. Round the free edges with scissors. Open up the paper, and mark folds clockwise: North, North-North-East, North-East, East-North-East, East, East-South-East, South-East, South-South-East, South, South-South-West, South-West, West-South-West, West, West-North-West, North-West, North-North-West, North—or simply N, NNE, NE, ENE, E, ESE, SE, SSE, S, SSW, SW, WSW, W, WNW, NW, NNW, N. Place this circular piece

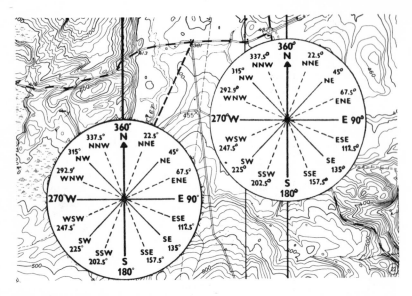

You can turn your folded-paper circle into a simple protractor by providing it with the degree numbers of a circle. Zero and 360 degrees coincide.

of paper with its center directly over your "base of operations," and with the fold marked North lying north on the meridian line that runs through your spot. Now, to go in different directions from your base, you may follow the fold marked NE and continue into the landscape along this north-east "road," or you can go south-south-west, or in any of the other directions (see illustration on page 27).

From Paper Circle to Protractor

The paper circle with its sixteen direction markings is your first step toward using a *protractor*. As you probably know, a protractor is an instrument used for measuring angles. It consists of a circle made from a piece of metal or plastic marked in the 360 degrees of the full circle. The markings start with 0 degrees, go clockwise around, and wind up at the 0 degree mark with 360 degrees—0° and 360° coincide. Some protractors, for ease in carrying, are semi-circular only.

In using a protractor, the 0-360 degree marking indicates north. South is then how many degrees? 180. Correct! East is 90, west is 270. North-East is 45, south-east 135, and so on. With that information, you

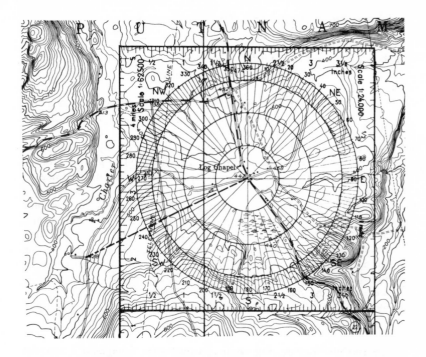

Use the transparent protractor from the envelope in the back of this book for practice in finding directions between various points of the map.

can turn your paper circle into a primitive protractor: just add the degree numbers at the appropriate direction names:

N – 0 and 360	NNE – 22½	NE – 45	ENE – 67½
E – 90	ESE – 112½	SE – 135	SSE – 157½
S – 180	SSW – 202½	SW – 225	WSW – 247½
W – 270	WNW – 292½	NW – 315	NNW – 337½

It is quite obvious that for exact degree figuring, your folded-paper protractor will not be very accurate. Your home-made gadget will assist you in learning the principle of the use of a protractor, but if you want to determine correct readings, you need the real thing. And this you will find in the envelope in the back of the book, in the form of a transparent, full-circle practicing protractor.

Finding Map Directions with a Protractor

Bring out the practicing protractor from the envelope in the back of the book, and learn to use it for taking degree readings.

Let us say that you want to go exploring in various directions out of your "base of operations."

Place the center of your practicing protractor on the base, and line up the protractor's north-south line (its 360-180 diameter) parallel with the nearest north-south (meridian line) of the map, with the protractor's 360 marking to the north. You are all set now. For any direction you want to go, you start at the center, at the point you've picked, proceed from here over the degree mark you have decided on, and continue on your way.

But you may not want to go in any arbitrary direction at all. You may want to go from "here" to "there." What direction is it? Again, center the protractor on your starting point—the "here"—and line up the 360-180 diameter parallel to the nearest meridian line, with the 360° marking to the north. Now lay a ruler or the edge of a piece of paper from the starting point to your destination—to the "there." Read the number of degrees where the edge of the ruler or the paper cuts the circle of the protractor. That's the direction in which you want to go, expressed in degrees (see illustration on page 29).

Protractor Practice—Become accustomed to think of directions in terms of degrees, by using your practicing protractor.

TAKE POINT BEARINGS INDOOR PRACTICE

PURPOSE—To become acquainted with the use of a protractor for determining directions on a map.

TEST YOURSELF—On page 31 you will find a schematic map showing a number of locations with their relationship to each other and to north as represented by several meridian lines. Using your practicing protractor, determine the degree readings between the following points:

1. From 1 (Church) to 2 (Lake) . . . . . °   6. From 4 to 2. . . °
2. From 2 (Lake) to 3 (Hill) . . . . . °   7. From 1 to 6. . . °
3. From 3 (Hill) to 4 (Quarry) . . . . . °   8. From 5 to 1. . . °
4. From 4 (Quarry) to 5 (Bridge) . . . . °   9. From 3 to 6. . . °
5. From 5 (Bridge) to 6 (Cemetery) . . . °   10. From 2 to 4. . . °

(Answers are found on page 131.)

AS GAME—Provide each player with a mimeographed sheet copied

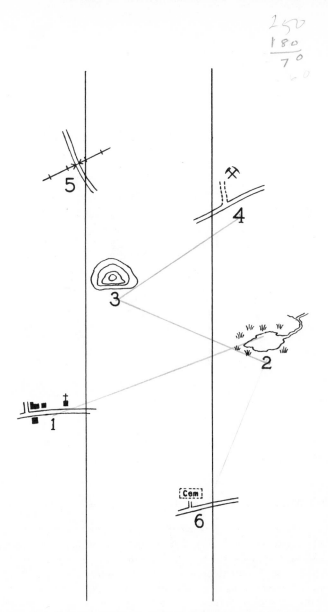

Read instructions for this practice on page 30. Using the practicing protractor from the envelope in the back of the book, determine the directions between the points listed. Parallel lines are north-south meridians.

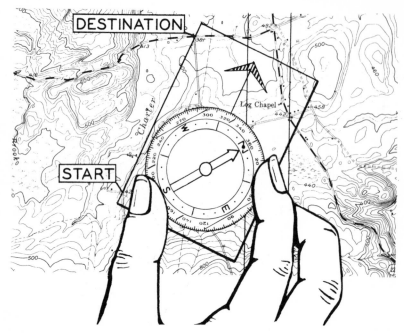

FIRST STEP in using Orienteering compass as protractor: Place base plate on map in such a way that one edge touches·start and destination both.

from page 31, pencil, and a practicing protractor (from Orienteering Kit, see page 133). Give the players 10 minutes in which to do the job. Player with most correct answers within the time limit wins.

Finding Map Directions with an Orienteering Compass

In the modern Orienteering compass, the circular compass housing is attached to a rectangular base plate in such a way that it can be turned. This adds a protractor-ruler feature to the compass' regular function.

When you use an Orienteering compass for determining map directions, the compass housing with its 360 degree markings becomes your protractor, the base plate with its straight sides your ruler. Since the compass needle plays no part in the job of using the Orienteering compass as a protractor-ruler, you can get along for this purpose with a needle-free Orienteering compass—and that's exactly what the training compass

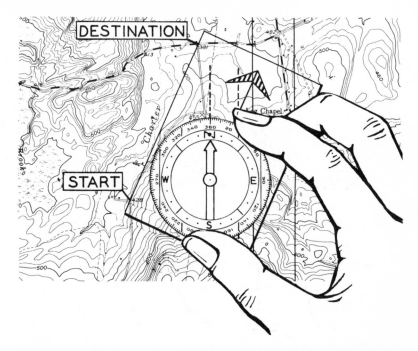

SECOND STEP in using Orienteering compass as protractor: Turn housing with orienting arrow parallel to meridian. Read degrees at base of direction line.

is, which you will find in the envolope at the back of this book. Get out that training compass and learn the "slick-trick" method by which it will give you the map directions you seek:

Place the training compass on the map in such a way that one edge of the base plate touches your starting point and your destination both, with the direction-of-travel arrowhead on the base plate pointing in the direction of the destination.

Now, turn the compass housing with its 360 degree markings until the orienting arrow which is printed on it points to north on the map — that is, lies parallel to the nearest north-south meridian line with the arrow point toward north.

Your compass is now "set," and all you have to do to get the direction is to look at the degree marking on the rim of the compass housing where the direction line touches it. There is your direction in degrees! Easy? It sure is — with an Orienteering compass, or a "reasonable facsimile"!

Orienteering Compass as Protractor — The training compass gives you the means for practice in using compass as protractor.

PURPOSE — Practice in determining degree directions on an actual map with the protractor-ruler of the Orienteering compass.

TEST YOURSELF — Open up the training map, and take out the training compass from the envelope in the back of the book. Then find the directions in degrees between the following points:

1. From road-T in Glenburnie to top of Record Hill . . . . . .° _359_

2. From Record Hill to crossroad south of BM 474 . . . . . .° _92_

3. From crossroad south of BM 474 to Camp Adirondack . . . . . .° _257_

4. From Camp Adirondack to Log Chapel . . . . . .°

5. From Log Chapel to Meadow Knoll Cemetery . . . . . .°

(The correct answers are found on page 131).

AS GAME — Provide each player with a training map and a training compass (from Orienteering Training Kit, see page 133). Then take each direction separately: "What is the direction in degrees from the road-T in Glenburnie to the top of Record Hill?" As soon as a player has determined the degrees, he holds up a hand. If correct within five degrees, he scores 20 points; if wrong, next player has a chance to score. And so on, up to 100 points for all answers correct.

Distances

The scales in the bottom margin of your map give you the means for measuring distances on the map. These scales are usually given in four ways: (1) As a fraction — 1:24,000 or 1:62,500; (2) as a ruler divided into miles and fractions of a mile; (3) as a ruler divided into thousands of feet; and (4) as a ruler divided into kilometers and fractions of kilometers.

On a map in the scale of 1:24,000, you know that 1 inch on any ordinary ruler represents 2,000 feet in the field. So you simply measure the number of inches and multiply by 2,000 to get the distance in feet. It is even simpler with the map in the scale 1:62,500, where the number of inches on the ruler gives you directly the number of miles on the ground.

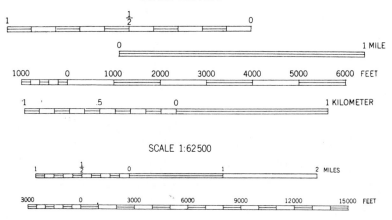

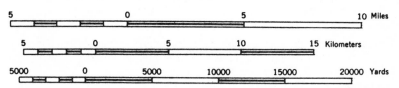

The distance rulers of the three most common map scales, as shown in bottom margin of topographic maps. Copy to edge of paper for measuring.

To use the scale ruler on the map itself, mark off the map distance between the two points for which you want to find the actual distance, along the edge of a piece of paper, then measure against the scale ruler in the bottom margin of the map. Or copy the scale on the map along the edge of a piece of paper and use this home-made ruler.

Orienteering Compass as Ruler

Even simpler: Use the base plate of your Orienteering compass for measuring.

On some Orienteering compasses, the base plate is marked in inches and millimeters.

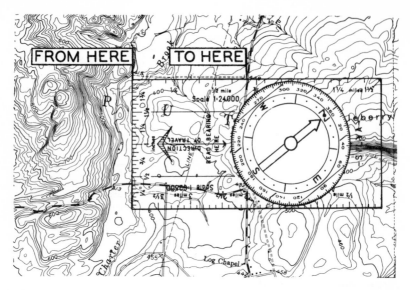

Some models of Orienteering compasses have distance rulers printed along two edges of base plate. This simplifies job of taking map measurements.

Others — such as your training compass — carry 1:24,000 and 1:62,500 scales for direct reading, as shown in illustration above.

Map Measurers

Another method for measuring distances on the map is to use a map measurer. This has a small wheel with which you follow on the map the road between your two points. The wheel is geared to a hand that turns around on a dial on which you can read the distance directly in the circle of figures for your particular map scale.

Distance Measuring — Practice distance measuring until you reach the point where you can look at your map and judge distances on it with fair accuracy.

DISTANCE QUIZ   INDOOR PRACTICE

PURPOSE — Practice in measuring distances on the map.

TEST YOURSELF — Transfer the scale rule on thr training map to the edge of a piece of paper or a cardboard strip or use the practicing compass to find, on the training map, the crow-flight distances in feet between the following points:

1. From Log Chapel to Meadow Knoll Cemetery . 7,000 . feet
2. From Meadow Knoll Cemetery to top of Hutton Hill . . . . feet
3. From top of Hutton Hill to Glenburnie . . . . . . feet
4. From Glenburnie to top of Record Hill . . . . . . feet
5. From top of Record Hill to Log Chapel . . . . . . feet

(You will find the answers on page 131.)

AS GAME—Each player has strip of paper or cardboard, pencil, and training map (in Orienteering Training Kit, see page 133). Leader asks, "What is the distance from the Log Chapel to Meadow Knoll Cemetery?" First player with correct answer within fifty feet scores 20 points; up to 100 points for correct answers to all five questions.

Designations

Place Name Designations

Places and other map features are designated by name in various lettering styles.

Regular Roman (upright) type is used for places, boundary lines, area names, while hydrographic names are in Italics (slanting type).

Place, feature, boundary line, and area names

Richview, Union Sch, MADISON CO, C E D A R

Public works—Descriptive notes

ST LOUIS, ROAD, BELLE STREET, Tunnel - Golf Course, Radio Tower

Control data—Elevation figures—Contour numbers

Florey Knob, BM 1333, VABM 1217-5806-5500

Hypsographic names

Man Island, Burton Point, HEAD MOUNTAIN

Hydrographic names

Head Harbor, Wood River, NIAGARA RIVER

Place names are printed in varying lettering styles to make it more easy to determine what kind of landscape feature is referred to.

Hysographic names are given in block letters, names of public works and special descriptive notes in leaning block letters (see illustration page 37).

Designation of Unmarked Locations

There will probably be many occasions when you'll need to indicate to someone else an exact location on the map not actually designated with a place name. The simplest way to do this is to make use of the place name that is closest to the location.

Let's take an example: Look at the training map in the back of the book. Find the place name "Huckleberry Mtn" (Mountain). Then locate the "Crossroads 1½ inches South-West of the letter 'H' in Huckleberry Mtn" (or we could write it simply "Crossroads 1½″ SW **H** in Huckleberry Mtn"—underlining the letter we want to indicate). All you have to do now is to measure from the bottom edge of the letter H 1½ inches (taken from the scale ruler in the margin of the map, or a regular ruler, or the ruler along the side of an Orienteering compass), in a south-westerly direction, and there is the crossroads. In other words: Find place name, then letter, then distance, and direction.

The distances are measured from that part of the letter that is closest to the location you want to designate—that is, the bottom edge of the letter if you want to measure in a general southerly direction, the top edge if you are measuring north, left edge if west, right edge if east, and so on.

Place Location Practice—In addition to practice below, figure out for yourself how you would describe other locations in Orienteering "language."

FIND PLACES ON THE MAP   INDOOR PRACTICE

PURPOSE—To familiarize yourself with the method for designating unmarked locations on the map.

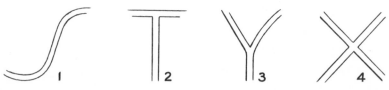

Terms used in describing road locations add up to STYX: 1. Road bend. 2. Road-T. 3. Road-Y or road fork. 4. Crossroads or Road-X.

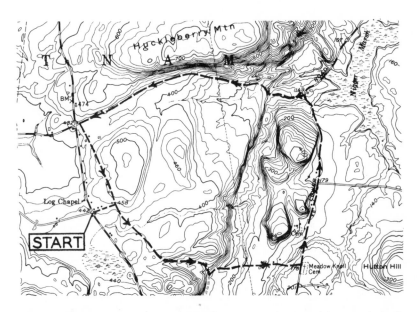

Follow imaginary map "walk" described on pages 40-46, on training map in back of book. Begin at START, proceed in counter-clockwise direction.

TEST YOURSELF — Locate the following places on the training map, and write down on the dotted lines what they are:

1. 2" S R in Record Hill...... *Glenburne T* ....
2. ³/₄" E e in Charter Brook ....*X 455* ....
3. 1⁵/₈" SE U in PUTNAM ....
4. 1³/₁₆" WNW H in Hutton Hill.............................
5. 1¹/₈" N l in Log Chapel.................................
6. ⁵/₈" NW M in Meadow Knoll Cem.........................
7. ¹/₄" N k in Sucker Brook.................................
8. 1¹/₂" NE l in Record Hill.................................
9. ⁵/₈" W L in Log Chapel.................................
10. ⁷/₈" S l in Huckleberry Mtn.................................

(You will find the correct answers on page 132.)

AS GAME — Copy above list on blackboard, OR give each player a

Compare map with landscape: Log Chapel on wrong side of road, road ahead bending in wrong direction, etc. Map is obviously not "oriented."

mimeographed copy to fill out. Score 10 points for each map location correctly identified; up to 100 points for all 10 places located.

TRAVELING BY MAP

Now that you know the features of a map, it is time to take a map walk. Decide on a place for starting your trip, lay out an appropriate route on the map, and try to follow it in the field.

Try an Imaginary Map "Walk" First

To give you the feeling of a typical map walk, unfold the training map, and take an imaginary "walk" on it.

Let's say that you decide to start from the crossroad south of the Log Chapel, and take a "hike" that will bring you in counter-clockwise direction—east, north, west, south—along the route shown on page 39.

Compare map with landscape: Log Chapel on correct side of road, road ahead
bending in proper direction, etc. Map fits landscape, is "oriented."

You arrive at the Log Chapel, then proceed south to the crossroads
and are ready to start out. But in what direction? Do you go straight
ahead, to the left, to the right, or straight backward?

Orienting the Map

The simplest way to know what direction to go on a map is by "orienting" the map. To "orient" a map means to turn it in such a way that what
is north on the map fits north in the landscape.

So you inspect the map and your surroundings, and twist the map
around, until the crossroads on it fit the actual crossroads, at which you
are standing, with the Log Chapel in its right location.

You have "oriented" the map "by inspection."

The whole thing is simple now. The road to take is to the left of
you. And to be doubly certain, you have an easy way of checking that it
is the right one: About 800 feet ahead of you, you should strike a road-T.

Determining Distances

800 feet. Well, how do you know when you have walked 800 feet?

The best way you have of determining distances in the field is *by your step* — or, even better, *by your double-step or pace,* counting off each time you put down the left foot — or right, if you prefer.

We have been doing it daily since Roman times!

Have you ever wondered why a mile contains the peculiar figure of 5,280 feet? For the reason that one thousand double-steps of the average Roman soldier at the time of the Caesars was that many times the length of the foot of that same soldier! The Latin for one thousand double-steps or paces, *millia passuum,* was later abbreviated into our English "mile."

This will give you a clue to the length of your own double-step. It will be in the neighborhood of 5 feet — and for general uses that figure is close enough.

If you want to be more exact, measure the length of your double-step for once and for all, and remember it.

For this measuring, lay out a step course: Put a stake in the ground,

For determining the length of your step, lay out a step course 200 feet long. Walk it twice, then divide number of steps into 400 feet covered.

NUMBER OF MINUTES TO COVER 1 MILE	HIGHWAY	OPEN FIELD	OPEN WOODS	MOUNTAIN & FOREST
WALK	15	25	30	40
RUN	10	13	16	22

You can estimate the distance you have traveled by the number of minutes elapsed. Various speeds and terrains influence time to cover 1 mile.

and measure out with a tape measure a distance of 200 feet. Place another stake here. Then walk from stake to stake and back again, counting your double-steps. Divide the complete length covered — 400 feet — with the number of double-steps to get the length of your average pace. If you covered it in 80 double-steps, your average double-step is 5 feet. If you used 90 double-steps, each double-step is close to 4½ feet.

Another way of determining the distance you have covered is *by time elapsed*. This is shown schematically in the drawing on this page. The times given here are for each mile covered — 15 minutes, for instance, for walking one mile along a good road, 25 minutes along a trail, and so on.

The Importance of a Date

You start walking toward the road-T — but before you reach it you are puzzled by a road leading off to the right. It shouldn't be there — it isn't on the map!

What has happened? Simply this: Your map, as indicated on the frame of it, was last revised in 1950 — and much can have happened since 1950, and apparently did. What happened in this particular instance was that a building lot was sold, a house put up, and a road constructed leading in to it from the road on which you are standing.

Which only shows how important it is to be aware of the last revision

Topography from aerial photographs by multiplex methods
Aerial photographs taken 1942. Field check 1949-1950

Polyconic projection. 1927 North American datum
10,000-foot grids based on New York coordinate system,
east zone, and Vermont coordinate system

EDITION OF
1950

Dates are important. Your map was correct when last revised—but don't be sur-
prised if changes have occurred—especially if you use an old edition.

date of the map, and of the possible changes that can have taken place:
A secondary road may have been improved into a primary road; a marsh
may have been drained on to farm land or may have been turned into a
pond; a forest may have been cut down; or a wood lot may have been
planted.

So, after you have set your mind at ease in regard to this un-mapped
road, you proceed—and, right enough, you hit the road-T exactly at
800 feet.

Along the Road

At the road-T you orient your map again and turn south-eastward
along the right "arm" of the top line of the T. Second-growth woods all
around you, and rather level land—as it should be according to the map
since the contour lines are far apart. You cross an overgrown brook, and
soon after the improved road turns into an unimproved one. The map is
right again—the thin parallel lines that indicate the road become broken
lines.

The road swings toward the east and starts dropping, then toward the
south with a steeper drop. You have reached the road-Y, coming in on
the left "arm." In the crotch of the Y, you change your direction and
go north-eastward along the Y's right "arm." You are in flat country
again, with a meandering brook, and with a small lake on your right. The
unimproved road gets better, and soon you find yourself at the road-T
opposite the Meadow Knoll Cemetery—a typical country graveyard
with a number of old headstones.

You orient your map again, then turn left, northward on the highway.
For greater safety, you walk on the left side of the road, facing the on-
coming traffic.

According to schedule, you pass an old country church at your left,
and a side road at your right. Ahead of you, to the left, rises a steep,
tree-clad cliff. How steep is it? Plenty steep—just look at those con-

Whenever you reach a prominent landmark or a turn in your route, take time to orient your map. You will then always know exactly where you are.

tour lines; they are right on top of each other. How high? Locate the number 179 on the map at the point where the sideroad strikes the highway—that's the elevation of that particular point. Now "crawl" up the cliff: You cross the light 180 foot contour line and the heavier 200 foot line, then several light lines, the heavy 300 foot contour, more light lines, and then the heavy 400 foot contour line. The 400 foot line is closed to indicate the top of the hill, but there is another closed line within it—the 420 foot contour.

You figure that the view from that hill should be pretty good and decide to climb it. You wouldn't want to climb the cliff wall, but the map tells you that the hill slopes up more easily from the north. So you walk up the road "apiece" — about 2,000 feet beyond the side road — and climb the hill from there. You were right — the view is marvelous down over the valley, over fertile fields and lusciously green marshes, toward distant hills.

Down, and northward again along the road until it swings north-east. There should be an unimproved road to the left here. If that's the road, it surely *is* unimproved! But it must be right, for there's a farm house and a couple of barns close by in exactly the same relative location to each other as the symbols on the map. You take a chance on the road, and soon discover that it is correct enough, for the cliff wall of Huckleberry Mountain rises high on your right as you hike along the lane.

Eventually, the road improves, and you can see cars whizzing by on the mainroad that lies ahead. But just before you strike the mainroad, you turn left on an unimproved road to keep away from mainroad traffic, and shortly afterwards arrive at a familiar point — the road-T you passed on the out-trip. A few feet more along the road to the right — the same 800 feet that formed the first leg of your journey — and you are back at your starting point, the crossroads south of the Log Chapel.

Now for an Actual Walk by Map

Your map walk was a fairly simple one — especially since you took it on the map without actually walking it!

Now get out the map of your home territory, plan a trip on it, and take an actual walk by map through your own countryside.

Don't be too ambitious the first couple of times. A walk of four to five miles should give you a good idea of the use of a map. You can then, later, be more ambitious.

Outdoor Map Practice — As soon as possible, get out in the field and make use of the knowledge you have just gained. *Indoor practice* is all right, but *outdoor use* is the "proof of the pudding."

LANDMARK HUNT   OUTDOOR PRACTICE

PURPOSE — Training in orienting a map and in locating landmarks.

GROUP PROJECT — Bring the group to a high station point of good visibility and the chance to see a number of different landmarks. Provide each player or buddy team with a topographic map of the area, a pencil, and a list of 10 landmarks to be located on the map, such as:

1. Indicate on your map, by drawing a circle around it, the point where you are now standing.

In the Landmark Hunt project, you learn to orient a map and to locate important landscape features on it. Pointers can be made from scrap wood.

2. Circle church approximately NW of here.

3. Circle crossroads approximately S of here.

4. Circle dam approximately ESE of here.

And so on, for 10 landmarks.

Set a certain time for finishing the project, such as twenty minutes. Score 10 points for each landmark correctly found and circled on the map; up to 100 points for all ten.

NOTE: Instead of using a list of landmarks, which at best can only be approximate, and also to add more interest, put up a number of markers in a circle about 30 feet in diameter, each marker pointing to a different landmark. These markers may be made of strips of wood, 1″ x 2″ x 10″, with nails to act as sights. One end of each marker is

In Map Point Walk you follow a route marked by colored streamers. Object is to locate and mark on your map certain landmarks passed en route.

pointed, the other end carries a strip of cardboard with a description of the landmark to which the marker points — such as "Church", "Bridge", and so on. The markers are fastened at eye level to uprights of 1″ x 1″ wood, or 1″ dowel sticks, with wing nuts. Players move clockwise from marker to marker.

Map Point Walk   Outdoor Practice

purpose — Practice in following a route and locating on the map landmarks found on the way. Map Point Walk is an especially good preliminary project for promoting a general interest in the subject of Orienteering. Almost anybody can participate since little skill is required, and because there is no chance of anyone getting lost. Also, any number of people may participate, from a small group to a very large one.

group project — On a map, lay out an appropriate route of two to three miles, leading through a number of easily definable landmarks. Then go over the route in the field, and mark it by colored streamers (one-inch-wide strips of red crepe paper) tied to trees, posts, or sticks at such distance apart that the next marker along the route can readily

In Map Point Reporting, each participant tries to find half a dozen or more landmarks, and to copy code letter or perform project at each landmark.

be seen from the preceding one. Hang a much wider streamer or a
regular Orienteering banner (see page 110), and place a North-point-
ing arrow marker, at each of the main landmarks on the route to assist
the participants in orienting their maps.

Send out the participants at two-minute intervals, each provided with
a map and a pencil. The object is to follow the marked route and
indicate on the map, by circling it, each of the color-streamered landmarks.

The scoring may be done on a time basis, the person with the lowest
number of minutes winning, provided his landmark indications are
correct. If incorrect, he may be penalized by having 5 minutes added
to his time for each error in marking.

NOTE: In case of a large group participating (twenty or more) it will
prove advantageous to station a judge at each of the landmarks and
have him score the participants for his specific location.

MAP POINT REPORTING   OUTDOOR PRACTICE

PURPOSE — Combining map reading and observation, to provide greater
enjoyment of traveling by map.

GROUP PROJECT — On a map, locate six to ten clearly indicated landmarks over a 2 to 4 mile long route. Then hike to the different landmarks and develop for each location a suitable question in regard to things found there, or terrain features seen from that spot — such as, what trees are growing there, what large buildings may be seen, and so on. Decide on an appropriate scoring value for each correct answer. Start the participants at two-minute intervals, each with a map, a pencil, and a report card describing the location of each landmark, the task to be accomplished here, and the score value for correct answers. The object is to score the maximum number of points within a three hour time limit. The participant decides for himself in what order to visit the landmarks and how many of them he feels he can manage to cover — he may decide, for instance, to locate first the landmarks that have the highest score value, and then try to cover as many of the others as possible within the time limit. The finished report card is turned in to the judge at the finishing point, and the score computed.

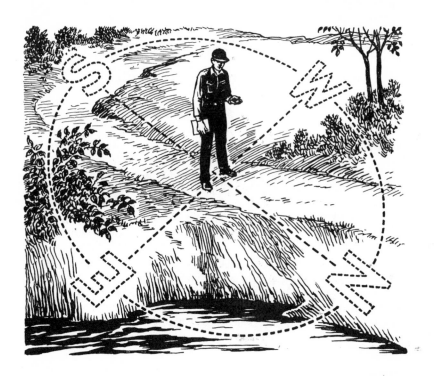

PART II

FUN WITH COMPASS ALONE

A great number of years ago—estimates say around 2500 B. C.—some
clever Chinese discovered that a piece of a certain ore, floated on water
on a piece of wood, would turn until one end of it pointed in the general
direction from which the sun shone half way between sunrise and sunset
—the direction he knew as south, or its Chinese equivalent. And if one
end of the floating ore pointed south, the other end obviously pointed
north.

Out of that discovery emerged the compass needle—a strip of
magnetized steel, balanced on a pin point, and free to swing in any
direction.

When left to itself, this needle eventually comes to rest with one end
pointing north. On commercial compasses, this end is clearly indicated

as the north end. It is either painted (black or red), or stamped with the initial N, or both, or formed in the shape of an arrowhead.

The Compass Needle Points Magnetic North

The force that attracts this magnetized needle is the magnetism of the earth. The whole earth is like a tremendous magnet, with one "end" in the north, the other in the south. The north "end" is the magnetic North Pole toward which the north end of the compass needle points when at rest.

If you belong to the kind of people who like things to be uncomplicated, you would want to have the magnetic North Pole coincide with the true or geographic North Pole. Unfortunately, it doesn't. The magnetic North Pole which attracts the compass needle is located about 1,400 miles south of the true North Pole—somewhere north of Hudson Bay and the northern coast of Canada.

That means that in Orienteering you will have two north directions to deal with—true north as it is shown on your map, and magnetic north as you find it with the help of the compass needle. Sooner or later you'll need to make these two norths jibe—but for the time being we'll concern ourselves with the kind of north direction that the compass needle gives.

Development of the Compass

After the invention of the compass needle, someone got the bright idea of protecting it by enclosing it in a metal case. In the beginning, this was a simple air-filled brass housing in which the needle swung around freely, suspended on a point—*air compasses* or *standard compasses.*

The next step was to find a way of breaking the swinging of the magnetic needle so that it would come to a quick rest. Different devices have been developed for this purpose. In some modern compasses, the magnetized needle swings in a copper-lined housing and in its swinging sets up electric currents which bring the needle to a fast halt—the so-called *induction-dampened compasses.* The most effective method used in more expensive modern compasses, is to fill the housing with a liquid that slows down the jiggling of the needle and brings it to rest quickly—*liquid-filled compasses.*

Until comparatively recently, the compass housing was marked with the thirty-two points of the mariner's compass. Then some other imaginative person suggested for compass indications the 360 degrees of a full circle. Because of this, the compass today shows 360 different directions or "bearings" instead of just the thirty-two of the old-fashioned "compass rose."

And finally, the conventional "watch-case" compass was improved into the modern *Orienteering compass* in which the compass housing revolves on a transparent base plate that acts as protractor and direction finder.

The Mariner's Compass carries the "compass rose" with the old compass direction designations. Modern compasses use the 360 degrees of a circle.

This type of compass has taken all the guess work out of direction finding and has made the use of map and compass together easy and accurate. The up-to-date Orienteering compass comes in different models — air-filled, induction-dampened, and liquid-filled.

Compass Point Practice — In the following pages, there will be many references to the sixteen most commonly used traditional compass directions. Before proceeding, familiarize yourself thoroughly with these compass directions.

COMPASS ROSE QUIZ   INDOOR PRACTICE

PURPOSE — To learn sixteen of the traditional compass directions.

TEST YOURSELF—Study the compass rose on page 53, then quickly mark the sixteen points on the figure on the bottom of this page.

AS GAME—Provide each player with a copy of the figure on this page. On signal "Go," each player attempts to fill in the names of the sixteen compass directions. Player filling in figure correctly in shortest time wins.

COMPASS FACING   INDOOR PRACTICE

PURPOSE—Quick review of knowledge of the sixteen main compass directions.

TEST YOURSELF—Stand in the middle of the room, facing one of the walls. Designate the spot on the wall directly in front of you as North. Now, quickly, in turn face North, then South, West, East, North-West, South-East, North-East, South-West, North-North-East, South-South-West, East, South-East, West-North-West, South-South-East, West-South-West, East-North-East, North-North-West.

AS GAME—Participants line up in open lines, arm-length apart side-

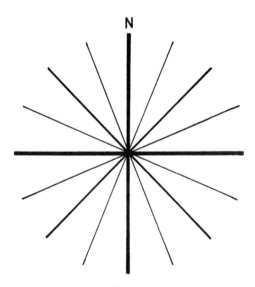

Study the compass rose on the preceding page, then get out your pencil, and write down the name of the sixteen traditional compass points.

Compass Facing is a simple game for practice in memorizing the main compass directions. It can be played indoors as well as out-of-doors.

ways and front-and-back. One wall of room is designated North. On signal "North-East GO!" all turn to face what they believe to be North-East, then, on command "Freeze!" stand motionless. Those who are facing incorrectly go out of the game. Then continue until only one player is left—the "champeen." OR let those who face correctly go out of the game each time, to give more training to those who know least.

TRAVELING BY COMPASS ALONE

The three main purposes for which you can use the compass alone—without the additional help of a map—are these:

1. Finding directions—"bearings"—from a location.
2. Following a direction—a "bearing"—from a location.
3. Returning to your original location.

Using the Conventional Compass

Let us say that your tool is the conventional compass—a magnetized needle suspended on a point in a compass housing marked in 360 degrees.

Finding Directions with the Conventional Compass

Let us assume that you are standing on some elevated spot or open ground and want to know the directions or "bearings" to various landmarks around you—to a distant hilltop, a church spire, a water tower, or what-have-you.

You face squarely the direction you want to determine, and hold your compass steady in front of you in one hand. With the other hand, you slowly turn the compass housing until the north part of the compass needle rests over the north marking of the compass housing.

Now sight across the center of the compass and read the number of degrees on the compass housing directly opposite to your face.

There you have the direction toward the landmark, expressed in degrees.

It is obvious that this kind of sighting and reading will give you a very crude specification that may vary a number of degrees in either direction. That is why the better compasses of the watch-case type are provided with a sighting device containing a lens ("lensatic" compass), or a prism ("prismatic" compass) through which the reading is done. But those devices increase the cost substantially without materially adding to the usefulness of the compass.

Following a Direction with the Conventional Compass

Let's say that you want to explore the distant hilltop you can see from the location where you are standing, and decide to reach it by traveling cross-country through the landscape that lies before you.

You determine the bearing to your destination by the method described in the preceding paragraphs, and find it to be, say, 140°. Remember that number! Or, even better, jot it down some place—for sooner or later you will start wondering whether you remember it correctly or not.

You start walking toward your destination. In the beginning it is easy—you can see it right there ahead of you. But suddenly it disappears! You have been walking down a slope, and the trees in front of you block off the view. This is where you start "flying blind"—using the compass only.

The direction in which you have to travel by compass is 140°. You hold the compass in the palm of your hand with the compass housing turned in such a way that its 140° marking is directly opposite to your face, on the other side of the compass center. You rotate your whole body until you have the compass "oriented"—that is, until the north part of the compass needle comes to rest pointing at the 360° north marking of the compass housing.

Now sight through the center of the compass and through the 140°

Conventional compass is generally of the "watch-case" type. Compass is oriented when north part of needle lies over north arrow on bottom of case.

marking of the compass housing. Notice some landmark in that direction —a large rock, a prominent tree—then walk to this landmark. Here, take the same bearing toward another landmark—and continue in this way until you reach your destination.

Returning to Original Location

After you have had your fill of exploring around your destination, you are ready for the return journey.

You traveled out in the direction of 140°. To determine the bearing of your return direction, your "back bearing," you add 180°—the number of degrees of a half circle—and get for your result 320°. (If the number of degrees of your original direction had been larger than 180°, you would have *subtracted* 180° from it instead of adding them.)

Again, remember carefully the number of degrees—320°—of your return journey. As before, better jot it down just to be sure. Then set out for home:

Use your compass as before, holding it in the palm of your hand, with the 320 marking directly opposite to your face, on the other side of the compass center, turn your body until the compass is oriented with the north point of the compass needle pointing to the north marking of the compass case, and sight toward the first landmark of your return journey.

If you have been careful in reading your directions and in sighting, you should have no trouble finding your way back safely.

Using the Modern Orienteering Compass

You will have a far easier time in your compass traveling if, instead of using the conventional compass, you use a modern Orienteering compass — the Pathfinder, the Rambler, the Explorer, the Huntsman,® or some other compass based on the Silva® System (see illustrations page 134).

The modern Orienteering compass gives you your directions directly, without the intermediate step of having to figure out and to check degree numbers. It makes it unnecessary to keep degree numbers in your head. It gives you the return direction without the necessity of adding or subtracting, thus eliminating the possibility of making a mistake in figuring that may have dire consequences. And when used with a map, the modern Orienteering compass combines compass, protractor and ruler in a single tool.

The Parts of the Orienteering Compass

The modern Orienteering compass consists of three basic parts: A magnetic needle, a revolving compass housing, and a transparent base plate — each part with its own special function, but all three working together to make an Orienteering compass an efficient and highly practical instrument.

The *magnetic needle* of the Orienteering compass is suspended on a needle-sharp point around which it swings freely on a sapphire bearing. The north end of the needle is painted red — on some models it is also marked with a luminous band.

The outside upper rim of the *compass housing* is marked with the initials of the four "cardinal points" — North, East, South, and West. The lower rim is divided into degree lines. The space between the lines on the housing represents two degrees. Every twentieth degree line is marked by a number — from 20 to 360. The inside bottom of the compass housing is provided with an arrow that points directly to the housing's 360° N marking. This arrow is the "orienting arrow." The compass is "oriented"—that is, turned so that the north marking of the compass points toward the magnetic North Pole—whenever the red north end of the magnetic needle lies over the orienting arrow, pointing

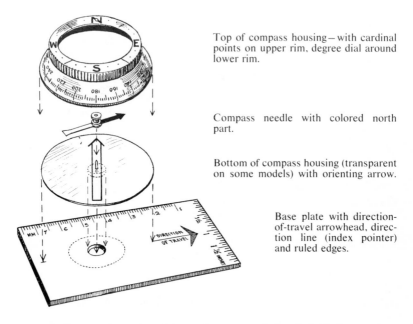

Top of compass housing—with cardinal points on upper rim, degree dial around lower rim.

Compass needle with colored north part.

Bottom of compass housing (transparent on some models) with orienting arrow.

Base plate with direction-of-travel arrowhead, direction line (index pointer) and ruled edges.

The parts of a modern Orienteering compass in "exploded" view.

toward the letter N on the rim of the housing. In the compass housing are also engraved several other lines which all run parallel with the orienting arrow—these lines are the compass meridian lines. On some models the bottom of the housing is transparent.

The compass housing is attached to a rectangular, transparent *base plate* in such a way that it can be turned easily. A direction line and a direction-of-travel arrowhead are engraved in this base plate. The direction line runs from the rim of the compass housing, where it acts as an index pointer to show at what degree number the compass housing is set, to the front edge of the plate where it spreads out into the direction-of-travel arrowhead. The side edges of the base plate are parallel to the direction line.

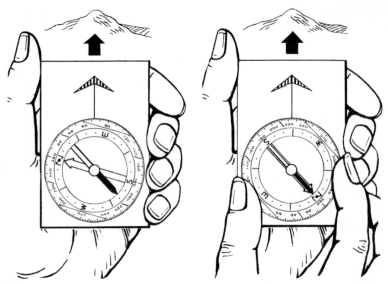

To find direction with Orienteering compass, point direction-of-travel arrowhead to landmark, turn housing until needle lies over orienting arrow. Bearing to hill 225°.

The side edge and the front edge of the base plate have markings for measuring—on some models inches and millimeters, on others the more common map scales.

Finding Bearings with the Orienteering Compass

Finding a bearing with the Orienteering compass is a simple matter:

Face squarely the distant point toward which you want to know the direction. Hold the Orienteering compass level before you in your hand, at waist height or a little higher, with the direction-of-travel arrowhead pointing straight ahead of you.

Orient your compass—that is, fit the directions on the compass to the same direction in the field—by twisting the compass housing without moving the base plate, until the compass needle lies over the orienting arrow on the inside bottom of the compass housing, with its north part pointing to the letter N on the top of the housing.

Read the degrees of the direction—the bearing—on the outside rim of the compass housing at the spot where the direction line, as an index pointer, touches the housing.

It is as easy as that with an Orienteering compass—no sighting over center and outside rim and chance of an incorrect reading as with the ordinary compass.

Following a Bearing with the Orienteering Compass

Let's say you're standing somewhere out in the field and have made up your mind to proceed cross-country to some hilltop in the distance.

You set your Orienteering compass for the direction in which the hilltop lies, by holding your compass in your hand with the direction-of-

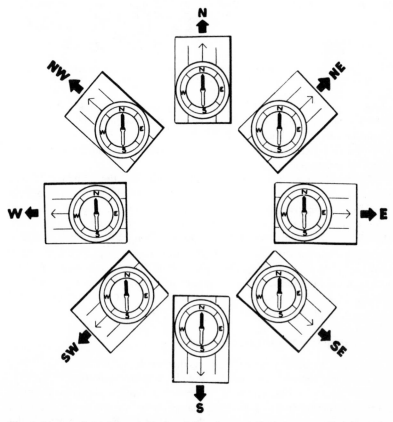

To go in any of the four cardinal and four inter-cardinal compass directions, set base of direction line at direction desired, orient compass, follow direction-of-travel arrowhead.

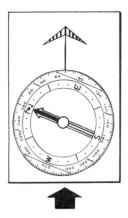

To go in a certain direction, set degree number opposite to direction line, point direction-of-travel arrowhead straight ahead of you, orient compass, and proceed.

travel arrowhead pointing to your destination and twisting the compass housing until the red north part of the compass needle points to the letter N on the rim of the housing.

You now proceed straight ahead in the direction in which the direction-of-travel arrowhead points.

If you lose sight of the distant hilltop, you hold the compass in front of you, orient it, and sight toward some close-by landmark—rock or tree—in the direction in which the arrowhead points, walk to that, then take a similar reading to another landmark—and so on until you read the destination. Only watch this: Do not twist the compass housing once you have set the compass for your direction.

What about compass degrees? What about figures to remember? You can forget about compass degrees and figures when you use the Orienteering compass—that's one of its great advantages. Your compass is set—there's nothing to remember! Just orient it and proceed!

Returning to Original Location

You have reached your destination, then decide to return home. How? Your Orienteering compass is already set for your return journey!

When you went out, you held the compass with the direction-of-travel arrowhead at the front of the base plate pointing *away from you* toward your destination. Obviously, then, the back of the base plate was in the opposite direction, pointing backward toward the spot from which you set out.

Make use of this fact for your return trip.

Hold the compass level in your hand in the usual manner, but with the direction-of-travel arrowhead pointing *toward you* instead of away from you. Orient the compass by turning your whole body (don't touch the compass housing!!) until the north end of the compass needle points to the N of the compass housing. Raise your eyes and locate a landmark in front of you in the direction in which the back of the compass base plate faces. Walk to this landmark. Orient the compass again, pick another landmark ahead of you — and so on until you have returned to your original location.

No degree figures to remember! No subtraction or addition with possible errors in calculation! No nothing! Your compass is set — simply use it backward!

Indoor Direction Practice — Before going outdoors, become thoroughly familiar with the use of the compass, through indoor practice.

FIND DIRECTIONS INDOORS   INDOOR PRACTICE

PURPOSE — Learning the use of the Orienteering compass for taking direction bearings.

TEST YOURSELF — Stand in the middle of the room. With the Orienteering compass, determine 10 different directions by the method de-

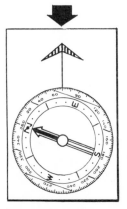 

To return home, do not reset compass. Instead, point direction-of-travel arrowhead toward you, orient compass, walk against direction-of-travel arrowhead.

scribed on page 60 — to door handle, for instance; nearest leg of table; right-hand edge of window; picture on wall — and so on.

AS GROUP GAME — Prepare for the game by writing on the floor, with chalk, as many numbers as there are players, and by fastening on the wall, with adhesive tape, the same number of numbered cards. Then determine the degree readings from each number on the floor to the corresponding number on the wall, and make a list of them. Each player has an Orienteering compass, a pencil and a piece of paper. Game starts with the participants taking their positions over the chalk numbers on the floor, one to each number. On signal "Go" each player takes the degree reading to the card that bears the same number as that over which he is standing, and writes down the degrees on his paper, and the number. On signal "Change," all players move up — player No. 1 to the No. 2 marking on the floor, player No. 2 to the No. 3 marking, and so on. When in position, another "Go" signal is given, and each player takes his next reading toward the card that bears the number on which he is now standing. And so on for five or more readings. Player with most correct readings within 10 degrees, wins.

AS RELAY GAME — Instead of as many chalk numbers as players, only one chalk number is written on the floor for each team. On the walls are fastened as many numbered cards as there are players in each relay team. Each team has one Orienteering compass. On signal "Go!" first player of each relay team runs up to his team mark on the floor and takes reading to card numbered "1." He returns and touches off second player, who runs up and takes reading to card "2" — and so on. Fastest team with most correct readings wins.

TRAVELING BY COMPASS

So far, it has mostly been "Let's say you're out in the field. . . ." It's time for you now actually to get out there to use the Orienteering compass. So bring it along and test your compass skill.

A Three-Legged Compass Walk

Try a simple test first, of a compass walk over a short distance.

Ready to gamble a quarter on your compass skill? No? Well, then, make it a nickel! Place a nickel on the ground between your feet. Set the compass for an arbitrary direction between 0 and 120 degrees, by twisting the compass housing until the direction line touches the rim of it at the degree number you have decided on. What'll it be? 40 degrees? Fine! The compass is now set for traveling in the direction of 40 degrees.

Hold the compass level in front of you, with the direction-of-travel arrowhead straight ahead. Move your body until the compass needle is

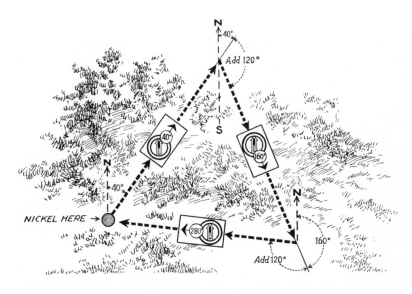

For simple practice in using Orienteering compass, try Three-Legged Compass Walk. Place marker, add 120 degrees to each setting from original.

oriented—that is, until the north part of the needle points to the N of the compass housing. Look up and decide on a landmark straight ahead of you in the 40° direction. Walk straight toward that landmark without looking at your compass for 40 steps—around 100 feet. Stop!

Look at your compass again. Add 120° to your original 40°—making it 160°. Reset your compass housing so that the direction line now touches the 160° marking. Again, hold the compass flat before you, direction-of-travel arrowhead pointing straight ahead of you. Move your whole body until the compass needle lies over the orienting arrow in the housing, with the north part pointing to N. Again, look up, pick a landmark in the direction of 160° and walk toward it, 40 steps. Stop!

Again, add 120 degrees to your setting of 160°—making it 280°.

Reset your compass, determine the direction to walk, and take 40 steps in the direction toward which the direction-of-travel arrowhead points. Stop! Bend down and pick up your nickel! The nickel should be right at your feet if your compass readings and your walking were exact.

How come? Look at the diagram on page 65. You have been walking the three sides of an equilateral triangle. When you finish you should be right back at your starting point.

Try this same stunt a couple of times, each time starting out with a degree setting somewhere between 0 and 120°.

Now that you have the idea you'll realize, of course, that you don't really need to stick to a starting direction between 0 and 120°. That was just done for the sake of simplicity. You can pick any number of degrees that suits you. You then have to remember that any time in your adding that you arrive at a figure larger than 360, you must subtract 360 from it to get your next direction. Let's take an example: Your first direction is 225°. Your second is 225° plus 120°, or 345°. Your third would then be 345° plus 120°, or 465°. There is no such figure on your compass—so you subtract 360° and get 105° which is your correct third direction.

Outdoor Direction Practice—When you can quickly and readily use your Orienteering compass, set out on simple outdoor compass practices.

SILVER DOLLAR HUNT   OUTDOOR PROJECT

PURPOSE—Practice in taking degree bearings and in following them.

GROUP PROJECT—The Silver Dollar Hunt is the Three-Legged Compass Walk described on page 64 turned into a project for a small or medium-sized group—such as a Scout Patrol.

Make up as many fake "silver dollars" (1½-inch circles cut from a tin can) as there are participants, and a number of instruction cards with distances and directions, such as:

"40 steps 90°—40 steps 210°—40 steps 330°"   OR
"50 steps 45°—50 steps 165°—50 steps 285°"   OR
"45 steps 18°—45 steps 138°—45 steps 258°"   and so on

(Notice that, on the same card, all the distances are the same; and that the directions start with a degree bearing less than 120 degrees to which are added first 120°, then another 120°—for the explana-

Miniature Compass Walk provides training in walking cross-country by compass. Very little space is required for putting up effective course.

tion, see page 65.) Scatter the participants over a field with fairly tall grass, or in a woody terrain with a fair amount of underbrush. Place a "silver dollar" at the feet of each player. On a signal, each player takes the first bearing and walks the first distance, then stops. When all have stopped, give the next signal. On this, each takes the second bearing indicated on his card, walks the second distance, stops. On the third signal, all walk their third distance and stop. On the fourth and last signal, all bend down and pick up the "silver dollar" which should be lying at their feet—or at least within sight—if the compass walking has been done correctly. Each player who can pick up his "silver dollar" scores 100 points.

MINIATURE COMPASS WALK　　　　　　　OUTDOOR PRACTICE

PURPOSE—The Miniature Compass Walk covers an area of only a few hundred yards yet gives excellent training in walking cross-country by compass.

GROUP PROJECT—The course for this game is laid in wooded territory by attaching a series of markers to the trees, each marker with its own number, and with the direction and distance to the next post.

The course is most simply laid by two people working together, each with a marking pencil. Tack marker No. 1 on a tree, and decide on a certain compass bearing. Write the degree number on the marker, then proceed in that direction, leaving your helper at 1, measuring the distance by your steps, until you reach another tree that can appropriately become Post No. 2. Yell the distance to your helper waiting at

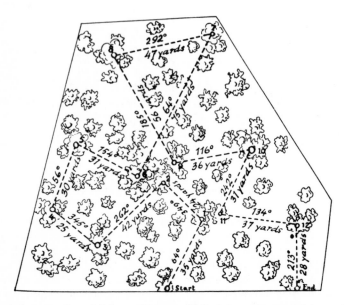

A typical course for a Miniature Compass Walk. It can be arranged in a school playground area, at a Scout camp site, in a local park.

Post No. 1, who thereupon writes this distance on the No. 1 marker, and joins you at Post No. 2. In the meantime, you have put up the Post No. 2 marker—on the back of the tree, preferably, so that it cannot be seen as you approach it—and have written on it a new bearing.

You follow this bearing until you decide on the location of Post No. 3. And so on, for about a dozen posts.

The participants are started with two minutes' interval, each of them provided with an Orienteering compass. Fastest time around the course wins.

PURPOSE—Training in following compass bearings and in measuring distances by walking. This type of compass competition is particularly suited for school grounds and camp site. The course can be set up quickly and can remain in location, and large numbers of pupils or campers can try their compass skills under the direct guidance of their teacher or leader.

GROUP PROJECT—Before the start of this compass competition, each participant needs to know the length of his step. So mark off a distance of 200 feet on the ground over which the participants can walk to determine the length of their steps (as described on page 42).

The compass course for the competition consists of twenty markers placed five feet apart on a straight magnetic east-west line. Number the markers consecutively from 1 to 20, with number 1 on the most westerly marker. An alternate, and simpler, method is to tie two loops in the ends of a piece of binder twine or other strong cord, 100 feet apart, and tie tags numbered from 1 to 20 to this cord, five feet apart. All you have to do, then, is to stretch out the cord between two pegs in an east-west direction, with number 1 on the west end.

It takes only a string 100 feet long, marked with tags at 5-foot intervals to set up a Compass Competition for school grounds or camp site.

When ready to start, each participant is provided with an Orienteering compass and with an instruction card telling him at what mark to start and how to proceed. You will find the instructions below for the cards of ten players. If your group is larger, either run the participants in several sections, or secure printed instruction-score cards for twenty players, at $.25 for the set, from the American Orienteering Service (see page 133), or from your local council of the Boys Scouts of America.

Start at Point 1

Go   36 degrees for 122 feet
Then 149 degrees for 58 feet
Then 235 degrees for 86 feet

Destination reached: No. . . . .

Start at Point 3

Go   38 degrees for 125 feet
Then 237 degrees for 90 feet
Then 186 degrees for 50 feet

Destination reached: No. . . . .

Start at Point 5

Go   22 degrees for 107 feet
Then 158 degrees for 54 feet
Then 186 degrees for 50 feet

Destination reached: No. . . . .

Start at Point 7

Go   34 degrees for 119 feet
Then 186 degrees for 50 feet
Then 228 degrees for 74 feet

Destination reached: No. . . . .

Start at Point 9

Go   346 degrees for 102 feet
Then 129 degrees for 78 feet
Then 186 degrees for 50 feet

Destination reached: No. . . . .

Start at Point 2

Go   17 degrees for 104 feet
Then 150 degrees for 52 feet
Then 142 degrees for 64 feet

Destination reached: No. . . . .

Start at Point 4

Go   36 degrees for 122 feet
Then 174 degrees for 50 feet
Then 228 degrees for 74 feet

Destination reached: No. . . . .

Start at Point 6

Go   3 degrees for 100 feet
Then 132 degrees for 74 feet
Then 225 degrees for 69 feet

Destination reached: No. . . . .

Start at Point 8

Go   346 degrees for 102 feet
Then 129 degrees for 78 feet
Then 211 degrees for 58 feet

Destination reached: No. . . . .

Start at Point 10

Go   343 degrees for 104 feet
Then 141 degrees for 64 feet
Then 145 degrees for 61 feet

Destination reached: No. . . . .

Each participant goes to the marker which has the number that corresponds to the starting point of his instruction card, and proceeds according to instructions. When he has finished, he writes down the number of the marker nearest to the destination he has reached (all the routes lead back to markers on the course line), and turns his card over to the judge. The correct destinations for each of the starting points are found on page 132.

If the player reaches the correct destination he receives a score of 100 points. Otherwise, the judge deducts from his score of 100 points, 1 point for each foot of error, or 5 points for each marker from the correct one.

Run the game three times, with different starting points, for a possible maximum score of 300 points.

COMPASS WALK   OUTDOOR PRACTICE

PURPOSE — Practice in following a cross-country bearing with precision.

GROUP PROJECT — After some practice using the compass, plan a beeline compass walk over a distance of approximately one-half mile. To lay out the course, locate a stretch of straight road lined with fence posts, or put up your own posts. Tack markers numbered 1 to 10 on ten of these posts, about 100 feet apart. At one of these markers — No. 4, for instance — face at right angle to the line of posts, take the

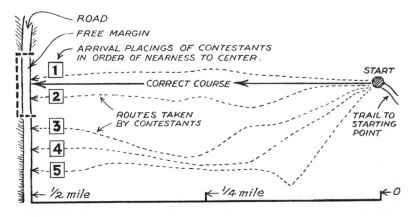

To lay out Compass Walk course, set out from Free Margin, hike ½ mile to mark starting point. Contestants begin at Start, must hit inside Free Margin.

bearing of the direction in which you are faced, and proceed in that direction as carefully as possible for one-half mile, or about 15 minutes.

Place a marker here. This is the starting point for the players. Then add 180° to your bearing if it is below 180°, or subtract 180° from it if it is above 180°. This is your back bearing — the direction from the point where you now are to the post from which you set out — and the bearing the participants are to follow to reach the correct spot.

Each player is provided with an Orienteering compass, is given the bearing to follow, and sets out. On a one-half-mile course a margin of 100 feet must be allowed for unavoidable errors. This means that any participant hitting the road between posts marked 3 and 5 — if your original post was No. 4 — scores a possible 100 points.

A Bee-Line Out-and-Back Compass Walk

After you have mastered the use of the compass with a fair degree of accuracy over short distances, you are ready for a cross-country compass walk — or "bee-line" walk, if you prefer.

Take yourself out into some terrain with which you are fairly familiar — your local city park, your camp, or some countryside you know. Decide on the compass degree direction in which you want to go. Figure on about half an hour's travel out (that would be about one mile), and the same length of time and distance coming back.

Well, you have arrived at your starting point. Set the compass for the number of degrees you have decided on. Then determine the first lap of your journey in the way that should be familiar to you by now:

Hold compass level before you, with direction-of-travel arrowhead pointing straight ahead.

Turn your whole body until the compass needle lies directly over the orienting arrow inside the compass housing, north end toward N.

Look up and sight straight ahead of you and decide on a landmark in the direction in which you are sighting.

Proceed directly to the landmark without looking at the compass.

When you have reached the landmark and thus completed the first lap of your bee-line walk, bring out the compass again, and sight toward the next landmark in the direction in which you are traveling.

Eventually you will have traveled the distance and the length of time — half an hour — that you had decided on, and you are ready for the return journey.

You turn about and do a back-traveling job as described on page 63:

For the Compass Walk, put up your own markers along edge of road, or pick a road lined with fence posts at evenly spaced intervals.

You hold the compass level in your hand in the usual manner, but with the direction-of-travel arrowhead pointing *toward you* instead of away from you. You turn your whole body until your compass is oriented with the north end of the needle pointing at N, raise your eyes and pick the first landmark for your return trip. And so on.

In another half an hour of back-traveling you are right back at your starting point—or close enough to it to recognize the familiar surroundings.

Overcoming Obstacles

On a cross-country walk there'll probably be occasions when there will be an obstacle in your way—a lake, a swamp, a building, or any one of a number of other things. Well, if you can't walk through or over the obstacle, you'll have to walk around it.

If you run up against an obstacle which you can see across, pick a prominent landmark on the opposite side of the obstacle and proceed to it . . .

If you CAN see across or through your obstacle it's a comparatively
simple matter: In that case, you locate a prominent landmark on the
other side of the obstacle, such as a large tree or a building. You walk
to it around the obstacle, and take your next bearing from there.

Before you set out again, you can make certain that you are on the
right track by taking a *"back-reading"* – looking back toward the point
from which you came. That point should be directly behind you – half
a circle behind you. You could reset your compass for a back-reading
by adding 180 degrees to the compass setting if below 180 degrees, or by
subtracting 180 degrees if the setting is above 180 degrees. But rather
than complicating matters for yourself with adding or subtracting and
later resetting to original degree number, make use of the direction line
of the base plate of your Orienteering compass:

Don't change the setting of the compass at all! Simply hold the Orienteering compass in your hand in the opposite way to that to which you
are accustomed – with the direction-of-travel arrowhead pointing
toward you instead of away from you. Orient the compass in the usual
way with the north part of the needle at N. Then sight *against* the
direction-of-travel arrowhead instead of with it and raise your eyes –

. . . then, after having walked around your obstacle, take a "back-reading" toward the point from which you started to make certain of your course.

you should then be looking directly back toward the point from which you came.

If you CAN'T see across or through the obstacle you can walk around it by right angles: You turn at a right angle from your route and, counting your steps, walk so far that you are certain that you are beyond the extension of the obstacle in that direction. You then turn at a right angle back on your original bearing and proceed until you are clear of the obstacle. Again, you turn at a right angle back toward your original sighting line, and step off the identical number of steps you took during your first direction change. You are now back on your original sighting line. You make another right-angle turn, and proceed in your original direction.

You can, of course, make these right-angle turns by resetting the compass at each turn, adding 90 degrees for each turn to the right, or subtracting 90 degrees for each turn to the left, from the original compass setting. But why do it the hard way when you can do it without any resetting whatever? You can do it by simply taking advantage of the right angles of the Orienteering compass' base plate:

Let us say that you want to go *to the right around the obstacle* ahead of you.

For your first right-angle turn, you then hold your Orienteering compass with the base plate *cross-wise* in your hand, with the direction-of-travel arrowhead pointing toward your *left,* and orient the compass in

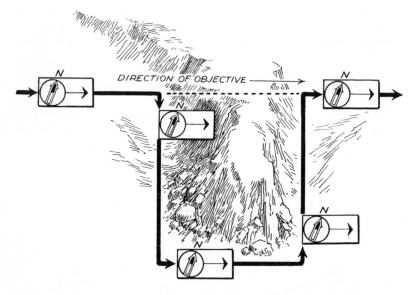

If you can't see across the obstacle, walk around it at right angles, using the back edge of the Orienteering compass' base plate for sighting.

the usual manner. You sight along the back edge of the base plate, from left corner to right corner toward a suitable landmark, and walk enough steps (count them!) toward the landmark to be certain that you are beyond the obstacle in its stretch in that direction.

For the second turn (to the left), you hold the compass the usual way, with the direction-of-travel arrowhead pointing straight ahead of you — you are back on the original bearing — and walk far enough to get well beyond your obstacle in this direction.

For the third turn (again to the left), you hold the compass with the base plate *cross-wise* again, but with the direction-of-travel arrow to your *right.* You orient the compass and sight along the back edge of the base plate — this time from right corner to left corner, and walk in the new direction exactly the same number of steps you took in your first direction change.

For your final turn (to the right), you orient the compass with the direction-of-travel arrowhead pointing directly ahead of you. The obstacle has been overcome—and you continue toward your destination.

If instead of going to the right of the obstacle, it is more convenient for you to go *to the left around the obstacle,* you reverse the instructions above and hold the base plate in the first turning with the direction-of-travel arrowhead pointing to the right, in the third turning pointing to the left.

Special Compass Uses for Fishermen and Hunters

For the sake of exploring, traveling by compass is in itself an exciting experience. But if you are a fisherman or a hunter, you can put your Orienteering compass to a number of other uses.

Finding a Choice Fishing Lake

Let's say that you are a fisherman always on the look-out for the best possible trout stream or lake.

You've heard of a wonderful fishing lake south-west of the Blackton railway station. Easy to get there and back with an Orienteering compass.

You have been hearing about Silver Lake from some other fishermen, and want to wet a line there yourself. Silver Lake, your friends tell you, is located directly south-west of the Blackton railway station. But as to getting there—there just isn't any road from Blackton to Silver Lake. You'll have to find your way cross-country.

Some beautiful morning, you take off. You arrive at Blackton station. And from here on it's quite simple with an Orienteering compass.

You know you have to travel south-west. That would be 225 degrees. So you set your compass for 225 degrees by lining up the 225 mark of the compass housing with the base of the direction line. Compass in hand, direction-of-travel arrowhead pointing straight ahead, you orient the compass, and sight. In that direction lies Silver Lake.

You reach it without difficulty—and Silver Lake proves to live up to its reputation. You get the catch of the year!

When you have reached your limit, you are ready to return to the Blackton station. That's easy, too. You simply backtrack by compass, and described on page 63, by sighting over the compass, but with the base plate's direction-of-travel arrowhead pointing toward you instead of away from you.

Relocating a Top Fishing Spot

You have been well satisfied with your success along the shores of Silver Lake. But the big ones, they tell you, are way out. So some day you get a boat and try your luck. You throw out a cast or two or three— and then it happens: You nab a really big one! You anchor the boat—that first big fish may be just a stroke of luck—and you cast a few times more. Another one, then another. There is no doubt about the kind of spot it is now! In a short while, you have your limit.

Obviously, that's a place worth remembering, worth coming back to some other day. But it is out in the middle of a rather large lake, and would be quite difficult to find again!

Or would it? Not with an Orienteering compass! It is simply a matter of taking "cross-bearings," writing down what you find, and using your notes the next time you come around.

To take cross-bearings, you pick out two prominent and permanent landmarks on land and determine the directions to them. What will they be? The large white house may be prominent, but is it permanent? Possibly not—it may be painted red by the time you come back again. The big tree? It might be cut down. The large cliff at the shore? Excellent. The boat dock where you rented the boat? Of course! If

When you've found an especially good fishing spot in a lake, make notes of cross-bearings to two landmarks, use them to find same spot next time.

no boat dock, you will have to decide on another permanent landmark.

Now find the bearing first to the cliff: You pull out your compass, point the direction-of-travel arrowhead toward the cliff, and turn the compass housing until the compass is oriented—until the north part of the needle points to N. You read the number of degrees on the edge of the compass housing at the base of the direction line. What is it? 113 degrees.

Next, you point the direction-of-travel arrowhead toward the boat dock, and again orient the compass. What is the reading to the dock? 32 degrees.

So, you write down in your notebook: "Excellent fishing spot, Silver Lake, 113° to cliff, 32° to boat dock."

The next time you decide to go fishing, you rent your boat, get out your notes, and set out:

The direction from the fishing spot to the boat dock was 32°. Obviously, then, the direction from the boat dock to the fishing spot is half a circle the other way. You therefore add 180° to the 32°, making it 212°. (If the original figure had been larger than 180, you would subtract 180 instead of adding.) You set your compass by turning the compass housing until the base of the direction line is opposite to 212 on the edge of the housing. You point the direction-of-travel arrowhead straight over the bow of your boat and have your rowing friend swing the boat about, until the north part of the compass needle points to the N of the compass housing. You raise your head and locate a landmark on the opposite shore — let's say a rock — and have your friend row directly toward it.

Now you reset the compass to 113° — the reading toward the cliff. You orient the compass in your hand, north part of the needle on N, and continue sighting over the direction-of-travel arrowhead while your friend goes on with his rowing.

You are almost there — the arrowhead almost hits the cliff. A little farther. Now! Out goes your anchor. And in goes your line. Up comes the fish — we hope!

Hunting in a General Direction

Instead of fishing, hunting may be your bent. Here also, the Orienteering compass comes in handy.

Let's say that you want to hunt in a north-westerly direction from your hunting camp. There were plenty of deer that way last year, as you well remember!

You set the compass at north-west — that would be 315 degrees — by turning the compass housing until the direction line of the base plate touches the 315 mark. You hold the compass with the direction-of-travel arrowhead pointing straight ahead of you, and orient the compass with the north part of the needle toward the N of the compass housing. The arrowhead points the way you want to go. As you walk, check with your compass occasionally to be sure you are holding to the general direction you had decided on.

When you feel you've had enough traveling for the day and want to return to camp, you check your direction again. But this time you hold the compass — *without changing its setting!* — with the direction-of-travel arrowhead pointing toward you instead of ahead of you, and backtrack as explained on pages 62-63.

"Pinpointing" Your Prize Kill

Some day you may be in real luck: You get that big ten-point buck you have been dreaming about! Your thrill remains after you have dressed-out the heavy animal. But how to get it back to camp — that's the problem. It is much too heavy for you to handle alone. You need help.

But finding the critter later would be like hunting for a needle in a hay stack—if it weren't for your Orienteering compass.

You plan your strategy: You know from your general knowledge of the lay of the land that there's a road half a mile or so south-east of you, and that that road leads to the hunting lodge where it should be easy to get assistance.

So you mark the location of your buck with something easily seen from a distance—by a white handkerchief tied to a nearby tree, for instance. Then you set your compass for south-east (135°), and start off, following accurately the direction toward which the direction-of-travel arrowhead points. You pick out landmarks on the line of travel and proceed from landmark to landmark. You count your double-steps carefully as you go, to be sure of your distance.

You reach the road—it took you 512 double-steps. You mark the spot clearly with some dead limbs, a log, or a pile of rocks which you can recognize later, then proceed to the lodge.

You line up your helpers (and possibly a pack horse or a jeep or some other conveyance if one is available), and travel back up the road until you reach the spot you have marked.

TO THE
ROAD

BACK TO
THE DEER

You got your deer—now to get help for bringing it out. You follow Orienteering compass to nearest road, later backtrack with same compass setting.

Now it's a matter of backtracking. Your compass is already set — you haven't disturbed the setting at all. All you have to do, then, is to follow the compass in the opposite direction from before, by sighting against the direction-of-travel arrowhead instead of with it. You sight landmark after landmark in that direction, and count off your double-steps. 512. Where is the deer? Well, you can't expect to hit it right on the nose even if it were a champion-size deer. But you should be close by it. You mark the point you have reached, then move around it in an ever-widening spiral. There's the white handkerchief on the tree! And there's the deer!

PART III

FUN WITH MAP AND COMPASS TOGETHER

Now that you know the functions of map and compass separately, you will want to use them together for your first taste of the thrilling sport of ORIENTEERING—the up-to-date name for the art of finding your way through unknown territory with map and compass.

There's real enjoyment of the out-of-doors ahead of you. You will get increased fun out of your outings as your trips take you cross-country, off the beaten track, away from the old, familiar paths—there are new things to see, new things to experience. And there is excitement, too—excitement in the uncertain: "Am I on the right trail? . . . Will I hit the tip of the lake? . . . Can I get through, or must I pick another route? . . . Is that my goal, right ahead of me now? . . ."

In the beginning, you may want to do some Orienteering on your own,

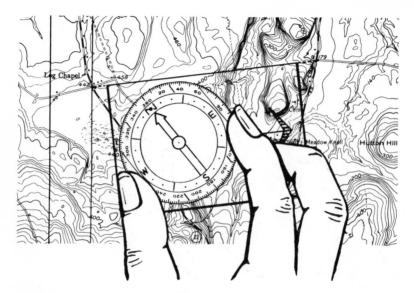

FIRST STEP in setting your compass by the map: Place base plate on map in such a
way that one edge of it connects start with destination.

but your greatest Orienteering thrills will come when you join forces with
other orienteerers.

Your First Orienteering Trip — At Home

Before you set out on an actual Orienteering trip in the field, let's see
what is involved by taking the trip first at home on the training map in
the back of the book. So open up the map, and lay a route on it.

Let's say that you want to start your trip at the crossroads ¼ inch
south-east of the letter "I" in Log Chapel — or, according to our map-
reading "shorthand": ¼" SE ' in Log Chapel. A short, suitable expedition might then take in the road-T north of Meadow Knoll Cemetery,
the farmhouse west of Niger Marsh, the crossroads north of the Log
Chapel, and back to your starting point — see map on page 87.

Setting Your Compass

Your first job is to set your Orienteering compass for the first lap of
the journey — from the crossroads south-east of the Log Chapel to the
road-T 1⅜ inches north-west of the **H** in Hutton Hill.

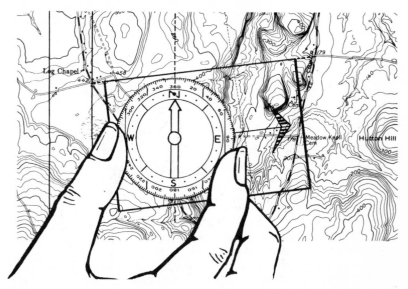

SECOND STEP in setting your compass by the map: Turn housing until orienting arrow lies parallel with nearest meridian. Compass is now set.

You have probably already bought yourself an Orienteering compass. This is where it gets a work-out! On the other hand, if you haven't gotten around to buying one yet, you can get along, at this stage of the game, with the training compass in the envelope in the back of the book. The reason that you can manage with the needle-less training compass is that the compass needle plays no part in the planning of an Orienteering trip — you only make use of the compass housing with its degree markings and the base plate together as a protractor, transferring the direction from map to compass.

Place the compass on the training map with one side of the base plate connecting the starting point at the crossroads with your first destination at the road-T, and with the direction-of-travel arrowhead pointing in the direction you intend to go.

Then twist the compass housing until the orienting arrow on the inside of the housing lies parallel to the nearest north line of the map, with the north point up.

Your Orienteering compass is now set for the first lap. What is the setting? Check the degree number at the point of the compass housing touched by the direction line. 84 degrees? Correct!

By orienting the actual compass in the field, then following the direction-of-travel arrowhead, you should have no difficulty hitting your first destination.

Next lap: From road-T to the farm house ³/₄ inches west of **N** in Niger Marsh. Again you place the compass on the map with the side edge of the base plate connecting the two points, and twist the compass housing until the orienting arrow lies parallel with a map north line, with north to the top. Your compass is set for your next lap. How many degrees?

Next set the compass from the farm house west of Niger Marsh to the crossroads 1⅛ inches north of the **I** in Log Chapel, and finally for the lap from the crossroads back to the point from which you started.

Your Distances

You now have the compass settings you will use on the way, but there is something else in which you should be interested: The distances.

So go over the route again to find the air-line distances between the different points. For this, use the inch ruler along the side edge of the base plate of your compass. The map is in the scale of 1:24,000. Each inch, therefore, is 2,000 feet. In measuring, you arrive at these results:

Crossroads to road-T N Meadow Knoll Cemetery	7,100 feet
Road-T to farm W Niger Marsh	2,700 feet
Farm to crossroads N Log Chapel	7,300 feet
Crossroads to starting point	2,700 feet
Total distance	19,800 feet

A distance of about 3¾ miles which you shouldn't have too much trouble covering in around two hours—unless you run into unexpected obstacles.

Indoor Map-and-Compass Practices—Use training compass and training map until setting your compass by map becomes second nature to you.

Compass Setting Quiz   Indoor Practice

PURPOSE—To become familiar with the Orienteering compass in setting the compass for different directions on the map.

TEST YOURSELF—Open up the training map and bring out the training compass. Locate the crossroads ¼ inch south-east of the letter **I**

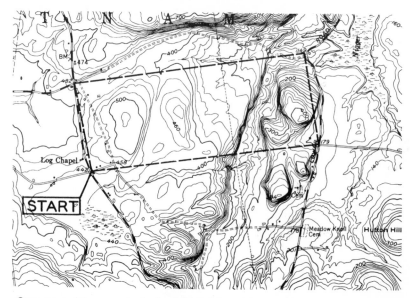

Open up training map in back of the book and locate the territory of the route shown above, of the trip described on pages 84-86.

in Log Chapel. That is your starting point. Now determine the degree bearings to the following points:

1. Starting point to Post 1, at church ⅝ inch north-north-west of **M** in Meadow Knoll Cemetery . . . .°

2. From Post 1 to Post 2, located at road-T ¹¹/₁₆ inch **W N** in **N**iger Marsh . . . .°

3. From Post 2 to Post 3, at farm house 1½ inches NW **H** in Huckleberry Mtn . . . .°

4. From Post 3 to Post 4, barn ⅜ inch NW **B** in Charter **B**rook . . . .°

5. From Post 4 to Goal, at road-T ¼ inch N **k** in Sucker Brook . . . .°

(Check your readings against the correct answers on page 132.)

AS GAME—Each player is provided with a copy of the training map, training compass (see Orienteering Training Kit, page 133), pencil, and a copy of the listing above. On signal, players determine the bearings. Player finishing in shortest time with most correct answers wins.

WHAT DO YOU FIND?   INDOOR PRACTICE

PURPOSE — Practice in making correct measurements and in determining compass bearings on the map.

TEST YOURSELF — Using training map and training compass, determine the landscape features located at these points:

1. Distance: 2,400 feet.
   Direction: 298° from **H** in Hutton Hill . . . .

2. Distance: 4,000 feet.
   Direction: 182° from **R** in Record Hill . . . .

3. Distance: 1,000 feet.
   Direction: 68° from **s** in Anthonys Nose . . . .

4. Distance: 2,100 feet.
   Direction: 174° from **U** in PUTNAM . . . .

5. Distance: 2,200 feet.
   Direction: 24° from **r** in Sucker Brook . . . .

(The answers are found on page 132.)

AS GAME — Each player has a training map, training compass, paper and pencil, and copy of the listing given above. Players have ten minutes in which to finish the task. Correct answers score 20 points. Player with largest score wins.

Compass Declination (or Variation)

For your first actual Orienteering trip let's just take for granted that the training map is the actual map of the territory in which you do your Orienteering, and that the route you have just planned is the one you want to follow.

You arrive at your starting point at the crossroads south of the Log Chapel. You open up your map, line up the side edge of the base plate of the compass to connect starting point with the road-T north of Meadow Knoll Cemetery and twist the compass housing to line up the orienting arrow with a north line on the map. You get yourself into

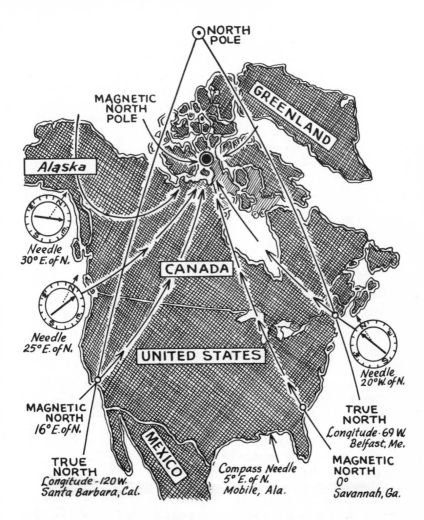

True north is the map direction toward the geographical North Pole, magnetic north is the compass direction toward the Magnetic North Pole.

start position holding the compass with the direction-of-travel arrowhead pointing straight ahead of you, the north part of the compass needle pointing to the N of the compass housing. You line up a landmark in front of you. You are all set to be on your way.

Or are you?

You would be if the *true* north of your map were the same as the magnetic north of your compass, and the geology of our continent didn't affect the magnetized needle. But unfortunately, they aren't, and it does!

The result is that true north and magnetic north are the same only along a line that runs off the East Coast of Florida, through Lake Michigan, and on up to the Magnetic North Pole located North of

TRUE NORTH

The magnetic force of the earth pulls the compass needle out of line with the true north direction. Angle between the two directions is the "declination."

Hudson Bay. On any location between this zero line and the Atlantic, the compass needle points west of the true north line. On any location between the zero line and the Pacific, the compass needle points east of the true north line. The angle between the direction toward which the compass needle points and the true north line is called "declination" or "variation." It varies from 20 degrees west (20° W) in Maine, to 30 degrees east (30° E) in parts of Alaska.

Locate your area on the maps on pages 89 and 91, and find the compass declination for your territory. Repeat it to yourself again and again, until it is firmly established in your mind. Then remember it.

If you are going traveling away from your home territory, check the compass declination in the bottom margin of the map you will be using (see page 25).

What Difference Does the Declination Make?

Why is it so important to know the declination of your location? Because you may be thrown completely off your intended course if you

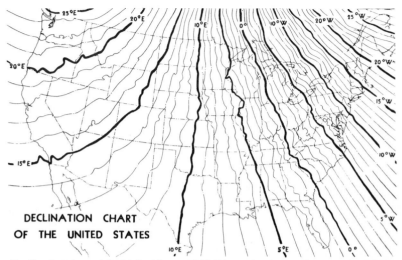

DECLINATION CHART
OF THE UNITED STATES

Declination chart of the United States 1960. Magnetic north and true north coincide on line east of Florida up through Lake Michigan. Other places have easterly or westerly declination.

depend on a compass direction taken from a map without taking the declination into consideration.

Let's assume a location where the declination is 15° W. You set your Orienteering compass, and blithely take off in the direction in which the direction-of-travel arrowhead points. Your course will be 15 degrees off! After you have traveled a distance of 3,000 feet, you will be approximately *50 feet off for each degree of declination*—a total, in this particular case where the declination is 15°, of 15 times 50 feet, or 750 feet! If you continue, you will be one-quarter mile off after one mile of traveling! No wonder you can't find your destination!

Fortunately, it is a simple matter on a modern Orienteering Compass to compensate for declination so that a wrong direction will not throw you off your course. It can be done in one of two ways: by resetting the compass each time you set it from the map *or,* what is much easier, by making your map speak "compass language." (Note: There are also Orienteering compasses with a declination setting device built in.)

Resetting your Compass for Declination

If your declination is WEST: Set your compass on your map in the usual way. Now find your setting in degrees at the point where the

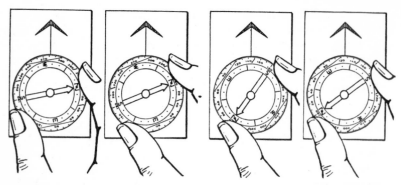

To compensate if declination is WEST: Check number of degrees at base of direction line. ADD declination, reset compass to new number.

To compensate if declination is EAST: Check number of degrees at base of direction line. SUBTRACT declination, reset compass to new number.

compass housing touches the direction line. ADD the number of degrees of your westerly declination to the number of degrees of the setting you read here, according to the rule remembered among orienteerers by the rhyme: "Declination WEST – Compass BEST" – anything is "better" when something is added to it. Then twist the compass housing so that the direction line touches the new number. The compass is now set for your map and your declination.

Let's take an example: Let's say you live where the declination is 9° W. You set your compass for a certain direction on the map and get a reading of 282°. You add 9 to 282, and get 291. You reset the compass to this new number (291°) and are ready to proceed.

But the declination out your way may not be west at all – it may be east.

In that case, pay no attention to the paragraphs just above. Instead, proceed as follows:

If your declination is EAST: Set your compass on your map in the usual way. Now find your setting in degrees at the point where the compass housing touches the direction line. SUBTRACT the number of degrees of your easterly declination from the number of degrees of the setting you read here, according to the rule remembered among orienteerers by the rhyme: "Declination EAST – Compass LEAST" – with something subtracted, the setting becomes "less" than it was. Then twist the compass housing so that the direction line touches the new number. The compass is now set for your map and your declination.

Let's take an example: Let's say you live where the declination is 18° E. You set your compass for a certain direction on the map and get a reading of 144°. You subtract 18 from 144, and get 126. You reset your compass to this new number and are ready to proceed.

Making Your Map Speak "Compass Language"

Instead of going to the trouble of resetting the compass each time you take a direction from the map, with the possibility of making repeated errors, there is, luckily, a much simpler way of compensating for declination. This way consists in providing the map with magnetic-north lines. By using these lines instead of the true-north lines of the regular meridians, your map speaks the same language as your compass. The settings you take on your compass using these lines do not require resetting to compensate for declination—the declination is taken care of automatically.

To provide your map with these magnetic-north lines, first draw a line up through the map in continuation of magnetic-north half arrow in the bottom margin of the map (to the right of the instruction map in the back of this book). Then draw other lines parallel to this line, 1 inch apart (see illustration below).

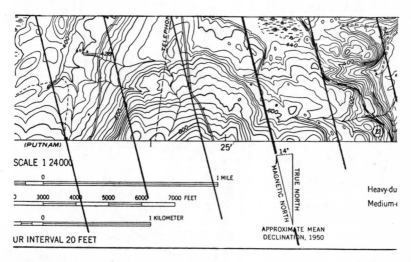

Make your map speak "compass language" by providing it with magnetic-north lines, the first in continuation of the magnetic-north half arrow, the others 1" apart.

TRAVELING BY MAP AND COMPASS—ORIENTEERING

Now that you know how to use map and compass together you are ready for honest-to-goodness Orienteering in the field. Start off with a couple of short cross-country hikes through easy territory, to practice up on your map-and-compass skills. If you live in some big city, you can do your practicing in one of its larger parks—provided you can secure a detailed map of it.

Then, later, get more ambitious and plan longer trips through tougher terrain. Finally, graduate into a full-fledged orienteerer, confident of your Orienteering ability and completely at home in true wilderness areas.

Getting Ready for Orienteering in the Field

For your first Orienteering hike, get out the topographic map of your local area, and shape on it a course to follow.

Choose an easily accessible starting point, pick four or five points in the terrain which you would be interested in hitting, and plan to wind

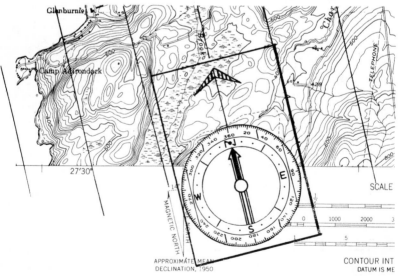

One way of orienting map with compass is to place edge of base plate parallel with magnetic north line, then turn map until compass on it is oriented.

up your trip at the place from which you started. Decide whether you want to take the hike alone, or whether you want to invite a friend along.

Then, at last, on the day you have set, you arrive at your starting point, rarin' to go.

But before getting under way, it will pay you to orient your map to get a general idea of the lay of the land and the trip that's ahead.

Orienting the Map with a Compass

Orienting a map, as you know from your map work (page 41), means lining up the directions of the map with the same directions in the field. You can do it "by inspection" as already described (page 41), but it becomes an even simpler matter with a compass. There are two ways of doing it:

Using Map's Declination Diagram — Set the Orienteering compass at 360°. Then place it on the map so that the side edge of the base plate lies parallel with the *Magnetic-North line* of the declination diagram in the margin of your map and with the direction-of-travel arrow toward North. Then turn the map with the compass lying on it until the North part of the compass needle points to the N of the compass housing. The compass is now oriented — and so is the map.

Using Map's Magnetic-North Lines — Set the Orienteering compass at 360°. Then place it on the map so that the side edge of the base plate lies along one of the magnetic-north lines you have drawn on the map (as described on page 93) and with the direction-of-travel arrow toward North. Then turn the map with the compass lying on it until the North part of the compass needle points to the N of the compass housing. The map is now oriented.

Using Map and Compass in Orienteering

While it is advantageous to orient the map at the start of an Orienteering hike to get the general lay of the land, it is completely unnecessary, when you use the Orienteering compass, to spread out the map along the route for the sake of orienting it. To get your bearings for Orienteering, you simply open up the map to that small part of it that contains your route and transfer the direction you want to follow from the map to your compass, without bothering about the way the map is turned. Obviously such a method simplifies matters exceedingly.

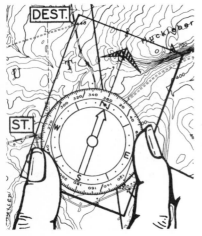

STEP 1 in Orienteering—On the map, line up compass with route from Start (St.) to Destination (Dest.).

STEP 2—On the compass, set the housing by aligning orienting arrow with magnetic-north line.

The Three Steps in Orienteering

To travel from point to point in the field, you follow the three simple steps in Orienteering: You place your compass on your map, you set your compass by the map, and you set yourself by the compass:

STEP 1. *On the Map, Line Up Your Compass with Your Route.*
Place the Orienteering compass on the map with one long edge of its base plate touching both your starting point and your destination, with the base plate's direction-of-travel arrow pointing in the direction you want to go. Disregard the compass needle.

STEP 2. *On the Compass, Set the Housing to the Direction of Your Route.*
Hold the base plate firmly against the map with your left hand. With your right hand, turn the compass housing until the orienting arrow on the bottom of the housing lies parallel to the nearest magnetic-north line drawn on your map, with arrow-point to the top. Disregard the compass needle. The compass is now set for the direction toward your destination. By using the drawn-in magnetic-north line you have automatically compen-

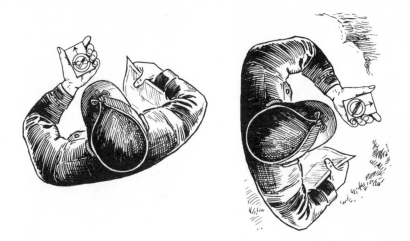

STEP 3 in Orienteering—In the field, follow direction set on the compass. Hold compass level in hand. Turn yourself until needle points to N of housing. Direction-of-travel arrowhead now gives direction to destination.

sated for any compass declination in the territory covered by your map.

STEP 3. *In the Field, Follow Direction Set on the Compass.* Hold the compass in front of you, at waist height or a little higher, with the direction-of-travel arrow pointing straight ahead of you. Turn yourself by shifting your feet, while watching the compass needle, until the needle lies directly over the orienting arrow on the bottom of the compass housing, with the North end of the needle pointing to the letter N (for North) on the housing. The direction-of-travel arrow now points to your destination. Raise your head, pick a landmark—a rock or a large tree or some other sighting point—in that direction. Walk to that landmark without looking at your compass or your map. When you have reached it, again check the direction with your compass on which you have been careful not to change the setting. Ahead is another landmark—and still another until you reach your destination.

When you have reached the first point of your Orienteering hike, you study your map again and set the compass for the next lap of your.

With compass oriented, raise your eyes and pick a landmark in the direction in which direction-of-travel arrowhead points. Walk to this landmark, then sight with compass to next landmark along route. Continue to destination.

journey. And so on until you have covered the whole route—until you are back at your starting point with a real feeling of accomplishment, your first Orienteering expedition a success.

Try an Imaginary Orienteering "Hike"

After you have done some short-distance Orienteering on your own or with a couple of friends, you'll surely want to try out your newly acquired Orienteering skills on a more ambitious scale. Then it becomes a matter of planning a map course through unfamiliar territory, of about five miles or more—depending on how energetic you are—and then traveling over the course in the field with map and compass.

To give you an idea of what you may experience on such an Orienteering hike, open up the training map in the back of the book, decide on a number of points you want to hit, and try to figure out how you would proceed from point to point if you were actually out in that area. As an example, let's say that you've picked the points indicated on the maps on pages 100 and 101—starting at the road-T north of Meadow Knoll Cemetery, and winding up in the same spot after a clockwise trip.

Clothing and Equipment

Now, if this were a real hike, you would, of course, need to consider your clothing and necessary equipment before setting out.

For comfort on an Orienteering hike, you'll want to dress in old, familiar clothes suitable for the season of the year. Pay special attention to your socks — no binding or chafing here; and to your shoes — no sneakers or soft-soled moccasins for this kind of activity.

For equipment, you'll need a topographic map of the territory, your Orienteering compass, watch and pencil.

You'll probably want to bring along a pocket lunch and a couple of candy bars for sustenance and quick energy, and possibly, during the summer, a canteen of water.

Your Outdoor Manners

Make up your mind in all your Orienteering to live up to the best traditions and manners of the true outdoorsman. In this respect, you can do nothing better than to follow the *Outdoor Code* developed by the Boy Scouts of America as part of a national good turn:

"As an American, I will do my best to:

"*Be clean in my outdoor habits.* I will treat the outdoors as a heritage to be improved for out greater enjoyment. I will keep my trash and garbage out of America's waters, fields, woods and roadways.

"*Be careful with fire.* I will prevent wild fire. I will build my fire in a safe place, and be sure it is dead out before I leave.

"*Be considerate in the outdoors.* I will treat public and private property with respect. I will remember that use of the outdoors is a privilege I can lose by abuse.

"*Be conservation-minded.* I will learn how to practice good conservation of soil, waters, forests, minerals, grasslands, and wildlife; and I will urge others to do the same. I will use sportsman-like methods in all my outdoor activities."

The Outdoor Code is clear in itself. A few of its points apply especially to the orienteer:

In traveling cross-country, you will probably at times encounter areas where fire hazards exist, caused by summer drought, down timber, dry leaves or grass or weed-stalks. A spark may set off a conflagration. For this reason it is a self-imposed rule among orienteerers never to smoke en route. Many of them go a step further and refrain from even carrying matches or cigarettes on their persons while Orienteering.

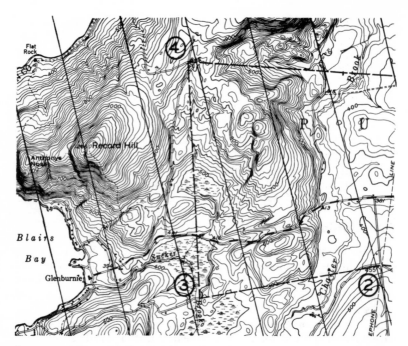

Open up training map in back of the book, and locate Orienteering route shown on these two pages. You start at S (Start), . . .

Consideration of property is of prime importance in Orienteering. Never trespass private property – permission will usually be cheerfully given. When crossing the property, *with permission,* don't walk over planted fields; leave gates the way you found them; leave farm animals undisturbed. When it comes to public property, heed the advice of "the man with the badge" – the park ranger, forest ranger, or game warden. Follow the regulations for the use of the area.

Be Systematical

Properly clothed and equipped, and with the best resolutions in the world in regard to your outdoor manners, you arrive at the spot you have designated as your starting point. You are eager to be on the way!

Not so fast! For successful Orienteering there are certain practices

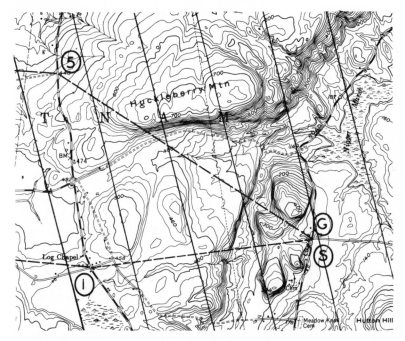

. . . proceed in clock-wise direction, and wind up at G (Goal). Description of what you will encounter en route is found on page 103-106.

which expert orienteerers have found of value. Better get into the habit of following them from the beginning.

So, instead of rushing off on your imaginary hike, you take your time and go about things systematically:

1. *Find your exact location on your map.*

That's easy for the starting point. You are right there at the road-T north of Meadow Knoll Cemetery.

2. *Find the exact location on your map of the point to which you are to go and check the general direction to it.*

You study the map. The first point you want to hit is located at the cross-roads a few hundred feet south-east of the Log Chapel – or, using map designation: ¼ inch SE of the I in Log Chapel. There it is, approximately 7,000 feet to the west of your starting point.

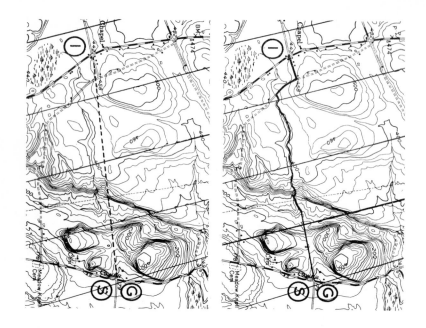

First lap of your imaginary Orienteering hike. Instead of taking bee-line, you follow
brook, then roads to first destination.

3. *Draw in the bee-line from the place where you are to the point to
which you want to go.*

Get out your pencil, then use the edge of the base plate of your compass
to draw in this bee-line.

4. *Decide on the most efficient route.*

Take a good look at your map. The bee-line from your starting point
to your first destination goes through a level stretch, then continues
downhill, across a brook, up a cliff, then over level ground. There are no
specific landmarks on that line to help you determine whether you are on
the right track or not. But by changing your course slightly, you will have
plenty of help: you can cross a brook and follow a tributary almost the
whole way to your destination (see maps above). And that is what you do.

5. *Set the compass correctly for cross-country traveling.*

You set the compass on the map from your starting point to the spot
where the tributary runs into the brook. What is the setting? 270 degrees – correct!

6. *Jot down the time when you set out from one point to the next.*
Your map gives you the distance between the two points, and knowing the distance you can figure out the approximate time it'll take you to get to the next point. When that time is up you should be close to your goal, and by watching your surroundings you should have no trouble locating it.

Off You Go!

Now, at last, you are set. You proceed on the route you have decided on from your starting point to point 1 of your Orienteering course.

The first stretch is up over a cow pasture, with steep hills on either side of you. You reach the crest of the pasture and run downhill now, through a grove of white cedars. At the bottom of the slope you find the brook, meandering along in slow motion.

You didn't hit the brook-T where the tributary comes in, but it should be nearby. Upstream or downstream? You study the map. The brook you intend to follow falls down over the cliff that's in front of you—you should be able to hear it. You listen. There it is—a bit upstream to your left. You climb the cliff right next to the gurgling water. It is a steep climb, but you make it. And then it is easy—the rest is level ground.

You reach the dirt road where it bridges the brook, jog north-westward to the road-T, then west until you reach the crossroads south of the Log Chapel. All along, you check your route on the training map.

You have reached your first destination according to plan. You are proud! You feel good! That first lap was really something. There's a bit of excitement in your blood now, and you're eager to be off to the next point—the crossroads ¾ inch on the map east of the **e** in the Charter Brook, about 2,800 feet in a west-north-westerly direction from where you are now.

You find the location on the map and lay out the bee-line. There's nothing to this one. The bee-line almost follows a road directly to your second point. You set your compass and yourself and are on the way. You reach the point in short order and prepare to proceed to point number 3—the road-bend 1/16 inch north of the **B** in Sucker **B**rook. You have a pretty long stretch before you—5,800 feet toward WSW.

For Speed: Use Roads

You draw the bee-line on the map. It crosses the Charter Brook, then strikes some steep slopes and skirts the tip of a swamp. Instead of following the straight line, you figure that it will be easier and faster to take the road south-westward to the farm house, cross the Charter Brook here (the farmer probably has a foot bridge over the brook which he will let you use), and continue between two low hills, and along the north edge of the swamp.

And that's exactly what you do. It turns out the way you figured it, and you arrive at your point number 3 with dry feet. Here you study what to do about reaching point number 4, for which you have picked the road-Y 1½ inches NNE of the I in Record Hill—about 7,200 feet N of the spot where you are. The bee-line to point 4 would be pretty tough: Through a swamp, uphill, downhill, another swamp, then steeply uphill along a stream. So, very smartly, you choose the roads instead—north until you hit your destination.

Then to point number 5—the road-T ⅝ inch NNE of the T in PUTNAM, about 7,900 feet to the east.

Cross-Country Next

This may be a real toughie—a mile and a half of cross-country going. You study the bee-line you have drawn. Maybe not so tough after all—not if you strike out for the brook, follow this to the farm house, then proceed south on the road until you hit the foot path, then east on foot path and unimproved road.

You set your compass for the farm house and start off. It's level ground first, but then it goes downhill, with hemlock-covered slopes on both sides of you. There, among a heap of boulders, you find the bubbling spring that is the source of the brook. You make your way along the stream through a carpet of ferns, then along grassy banks until you hit the farm house. You look out over the valley—this would be a spot to come back to: there's a beaver hut right down there in Charter Brook.

You enjoy the view but soon decide to continue on your route, south-ward along the road, then eastward along the path.

But where is that path? It should be right there at the road bend. Not a sign of it! Fortunately, you are prepared for such a situation by having counted your steps from the farm. The location is right—it's just that the path has been filled with a maze of undergrowth. You will have to go by compass and hope to strike the unimproved road that leads to point number 5.

You set your compass and continue. And sure enough, this is the path, for there is a foot bridge across Charter Brook, and a log across a tiny tributary.

And there is the unimproved road, and ahead of you the road-T you are aiming for.

One more stretch to go now—back to your starting point at the road-T 1¼ inches north of the a in Meadow Knoll Cemetery. How far? About 9,500 feet SE.

There's Always an Easier Way

You locate the goal on the map. The bee-line looks real rough. It climbs up over part of Huckleberry Mountain, down a steep cliff, continues over level territory, then down another cliff, up a steep hill and down on the other side. There must be an easier way to get there. There is! You decide to cut off a corner of Huckleberry Mountain and hit the unimproved dirt road south of it, then east on the road until you hit the highway, and finally south on the highway to your goal.

You set your compass at 146 degrees and continue your journey.

It is fairly easy going now, over bare rocks in spots, but from time to time among down pine, huckleberry bushes, and through brambles. You reach the dirt road—it is only a wagon rut, but a beautiful, shady lane with overhanging branches. And you are glad that you decided against climbing Huckleberry Mountain and sliding down its side—you pass a spot where you have a good view of the cliff: a sheer drop of close to three hundred feet!

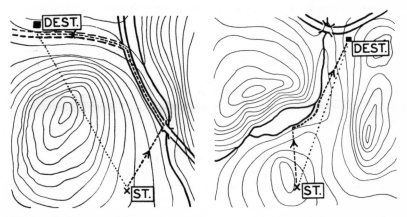

The good orienteerer picks most efficient route. (Left) Instead of climbing mountain, aim for bridge and follow roads. (Right) Strike for a "catching" landmark, such as a lake shore, to get closer to your destination, then go by compass from there.

It is easy going for the rest of the way. You don't even have to use your compass on this stretch—the map alone tells you where to go.

And so you finally hit the main road just west of Niger Marsh, and continue southward until you reach the road-T at the Meadow Knoll Cemetery.

Now for the Real Thing!

Your first Orienteering "hike" has come to an end. How did you like it? Although traveled in the imagination, it sounded like quite an interesting expedition, didn't it? Well, you would have enjoyed the trip a great deal more if you had actually covered the route in the field. So why not decide to set out on a real Orienteering hike at the earliest possible moment? By now you know enough about the use of map and compass to enjoy a fairly ambitious undertaking. So get going!

You will return home well satisfied with yourself. You may have made a few minor mistakes en route—but that's the way to learn. With each Orienteering hike you pick up new pointers—especially if you sit down after you get home and review your excursion, by taking a second turn over the route, this time on your map only.

And then there's another Orienteering trip to be planned—and another and another.

For there will be many more of them! Orienteering has entered your blood! In the future, the whole outdoors will challenge you to use your skill in finding your way across her widespread acres.

Then, Orienteering becomes far more to you than a new skill learned—it becomes your means of being your own guide in locating hidden fishing streams off the beaten track, in undertaking more ambitious hunting expeditions, in vacationing by canoe in some beautiful lake-land wilderness.

For although Orienteering, as such, is interesting and enjoyable, it is not an end in itself—its main purpose is to give you practice, practice, and still more practice in the proper and intelligent use of map and compass for finding your way in unknown territory.

ORIENTEERING RACES

Within recent years, Orienteering as a sport, in the form of "Orienteering Races," has swept Europe, and is well on its way to sweeping America as well.

Leaders and instructors in outdoor education have found in the different types of competitive Orienteering events a valuable ally in creating a

The start of an Orienteering race based on the route described on pages 98-106. Before setting out, orient the map to get an idea of the lay of the land.

greater interest in all phases of outdoor life, in addition to the teaching of map and compass skills. The result has been that Orienteering events have become regular features in many athletic and outdoor clubs, and are often arranged in Scouting circles by Boy Scout Councils and Districts, and by individual Scout Troops and Explorer Units.

The word "race" for this type of outdoor event is somewhat of a misnomer. It isn't speed alone that determines the winner in Orienteering. It is a combination of four important things:

Correct interpretation of instructions

Careful planning of routes to be followed

Intelligent use of map and compass

Time used to cover entire course

Temporary Orienteering markers can be made from burlap tacked to strips of wood. The size indicated is recommended for beginners' races. For national and international Orienteering events the markers are smaller (10-15″ high).

An especially fast runner may be off to a poor start by failing to follow instructions. Or he may be careless in his compass settings, or in making allowances for declina⁺ion, or in orienting his compass before racing off. Or he may run into unnecessary obstacles by picking a poor route.

To win in an Orienteering race, it pays for each participant to take it easy, to spend sufficient time in checking and rechecking, and to figure out the most advantageous procedure. This is especially true of the beginner. By the time a person has become an old-timer in the sport of Orienteering and has caught the Orienteering bug, his speed will have increased with his skill in using compass and map.

Planning an Orienteering Race

In order to initiate others into the fun of Orienteering, you may be instrumental in organizing an Orienteering race. The planning of such an event is not particularly difficult. As a matter of fact, it is probably easier to lay an Orienteering route than it is to follow one when once the main points of a successful Orienteering event is established in your mind.

Orienteering can be made to fit almost any kind of outdoor activity.

Permanent Orienteering markers can be made from sheet aluminum. Attach to metal fence posts. Paint red and white, with code sign or code number.

It can be a special all-day event staged any time of the year for a group of young people or adults. It can be the theme of a day of a Scout Troop or Explorer Post, or any other kind of camping group—whether boys or girls. It can be an easy activity for untrained or unskilled people of all ages, or it can be developed into a highly competitive event among experts—individuals or teams of two or more.

Whichever kind of event is decided upon, certain requirements must be met:

Suitable Territory—with interesting features but without hazards such as cliffs or dangerous bog territories. Permission from landowners to traverse their land—unless event is organized in state or national park, in which case ranger should be advised.

Maps—a topographic map of the territory to be covered, for each person or team.

Compasses—an Orienteering compass for each person or team.

Markers—a method for marking each station point, with streamers, or with special Orienteering banners or signs, each with a code number or a code design.

Judges—a sufficient number of helpers to function as starters and as controls.

Types of Orienteering Races

The type of Orienteering race to be scheduled depends on what the planners feel should be accomplished, or on the special interests of the group and the degree of its training.

Generally speaking, there are two main types of Orienteering races, although each of them adapts itself to a great number of variations:

> *Route Orienteering* — in which the entire route to be followed is decided in advance by the planners, and is indicated on a map at the starting point; and

> *Point Orienteering* — in which certain station points are established in the field and are to be located by each participant picking his own route from one point to the next.

Arranging Orienteering Races — A couple of persons working together can easily lay out the course for the average Orienteering race in a day's time. For running the event, have sufficient helpers available to man starting point and goal, and, if necessary, the individual stations.

ROUTE ORIENTEERING   OUTDOOR PROJECT

PURPOSE — Test of ability to follow, with compass and map, a route indicated on a master map.

GROUP PROJECT — On a map, lay out an appropriate route of about five miles, passing by a number of landmarks which are readily located on the map. Then follow the route in the field, and at each of the landmarks put up some kind of Orienteering marker, along the lines shown in the illustrations on pages 108 and 109. Finally, mark the route clearly on a master map and put this up on a bulletin board at the starting point.

Before setting out, each participant copies the route onto his own map, then tries to follow it in the field with map and compass. Whenever he arrives at one of the marked stations, he stops to locate the spot on his map and to circle the map location with a pencil.

Time has no bearing on the winning of this type of Orienteering race, but a time limit for completing the race should be announced in advance.

The winner is the participant who has found most stations and has indicated them most correctly on his map.

PURPOSE—Test of ability to select suitable route from one station point to another, and to follow these routes speedily with compass and map.

GROUP PROJECT—On a map, locate a number of suitable station points, then find them in the field, and put up a station marker at each of them. Decide whether (1) all station points are to be announced in advance to the participants; or whether (2) only one point at a time is to be revealed. If you decide on (1), you need to put up at the starting point for all participants to copy, a master map with all station points marked on it and with the order indicated in which they are to be visited. If you decide on (2), you need to put up at each station point a marker with information about the location of the next station—along the line of the illustrations on pages 112-113, which would be the station markers for a Point Orienteering Race over the route described on pages 98-106.

The participants are sent out with an interval between them of a couple of minutes. Whenever a participant reaches a station point, he copies the code design on the marker if the station is self-controlled, or has his map signed by the judge if the station is manned. The race is won by the participant who hits all station points in

```
THIRD  RACE  OF  THE  NONESUCH  ORIENTEERING  CLUB

DATE: Saturday, September 15th, 10:00 A.M.

MAP: Ticonderoga Quadrangle, 1:24,000
        N4345-W7322.5/7.5 Declination 14° W.

MEET: Road-T 1¼" N a in Meadow Knoll Cem.

DRESS: Long pants recommended. Brambles in spots;
        poison ivy in others.

SPECIAL NOTE: Permission for trespass has been se-
        cured from all property owners along route. Only
        conditions: 1. Positively no smoking - much down-
        timber. 2. Close any gates you may open. 3. No
        crossing of cultivated fields.

                        P. Jones, Secretary
```

Sample announcement mailed to members of Orienteering club for participation in race following the route described on pages 98-106.

```
┌─────────────────────────────────────────┐
│              POST 1                      │
│            W 7,000 ft                    │
│   Crossroads ¼" SE l in Log Chapel       │
└─────────────────────────────────────────┘

┌─────────────────────────────────────────┐
│              POST 2                      │
│            WNW 2,800 ft                  │
│   Crossroads ¾" E e in Charter Brook     │
└─────────────────────────────────────────┘

┌─────────────────────────────────────────┐
│              POST 3                      │
│            WSW 5,800 ft                  │
│   Road-bend ⅙" N B in Sucker Brook       │
└─────────────────────────────────────────┘
```

For a Point Orienteering race in which the station points are revealed one at a time, you need to put up a marker at each station.

the proper sequence and arrives at the goal in the shortest possible time.

Variations — Within the two general types of Orienteering races — Route Orienteering and Point Orienteering — it is possible for those who arrange the activity to use their imagination and thus add further spice to the event — such as in the following suggestions:

PROJECT ORIENTEERING   OUTDOOR PROJECT

PURPOSE — To test, in addition to their Orienteering ability, other outdoor skills of the participants.

GROUP PROJECT — Lay out a route as for Route Orienteering, or a series of station points as in Point Orienteering, and use method described above for actual Orienteering.

POST 4
N 7,200 ft
Road-Y 1½" NNE I in Record Hill

POST 5
E 7,900 ft
Road-T ⅝" NNE T in PUTNAM

GOAL
SE 8,600 ft
Road-T 1⅚" N a in Meadow Knoll Cem

For an Orienteering race over the route described on pages 98-106, you will require the series of markers shown above and on the opposite page.

As each participant arrives at a station, he is informed by a judge of a project to be performed at that particular station. The project may vary the whole way from writing down the colors of buildings seen from the station, or making a list of the trees found there, to the decoding of a Morse code message, or the building of a fire.

The score received for performing each project is added to the score of the Orienteering itself to determine the winner.

SCORE ORIENTEERING   OUTDOOR PROJECT

PURPOSE — A stiffer testing of a participant's Orienteering skills.

GROUP PROJECT — Score Orienteering is an elaboration of regular Point Orienteering. In this race, the stations set up in the field at various distances from the starting point are not marked in numerical sequence, and are not to be visited in any specified order. Instead, each point is marked on a map posted on a bulletin board with a figure that indicates the score value for reaching that point. The points most difficult to locate have the highest scores. A definite time limit for completing the race is announced in advance.

The object is for each participant to score the greatest number of points within the time limit. This he does by locating in the field the different points and jotting down the code letter or code design posted there, as proof of having reached them. The participant decides for himself how many stations he will attempt to find within the time available, and the order in which he desires to visit them.

If he exceeds the time allotted, a certain score amount is deducted for each minute he is late in returning to the starting point.

Let's Exchange Ideas and Experiences

Obviously, a few book pages can present little more than the basic ideas of this phase of Orienteering. So, if you are interested in organizing Orienteering events for some local club or youth group and would like further suggestions on this subject, drop a line to *American Orienteering Service,* LaPorte, Indiana, and ask for complete list of informative material, teaching aids, films, etc. For your convenience, a business reply card is included in the envelope in the back of this book.

Then, if you do run off some kind of Orienteering event, be sure to send a few words of comment on your experiences to the Orienteering Service. The exchange of ideas and experiences is of the greatest importance in the promotion of Orienteering as a sport. If in Canada, address your comments to *Canadian Orienteering Service, 77* York Street, Toronto, Ontario, Canada.

HINTS ON WILDERNESS ORIENTEERING

If you are the ambitious kind of an outdoorsman, you will eventually want to use your Orienteering skills for extensive traveling through wilderness areas—whether for exploring, camping, or in pursuit of your fishing or hunting hobby.

Such traveling is not for beginners. There are many related skills which you must master before you can undertake a sojourn of a week or a month through unfamiliar wilderness territory.

Training for Wilderness Traveling

In addition to the ability to use compass and map correctly in Orienteering, there are other skills that will be required of you if you expect your expedition to be a success:

Hiking Skills — For a short hike near home you need no special equipment and little hike training, but when it becomes a matter of covering an extended route it's a different story. Then you must know what footgear and clothing to use; how to walk most effortlessly; when and how to rest; safety on the trail; trail first aid in case of a possible accident far away from doctor and hospital.

Camping Skills — When your trip calls for spending several nights in the open, you should know how to take care of yourself: What equipment to pick and how to carry it; what food you need, how to transport it, how to prepare it; what camp site to choose, how to pitch a tent and prepare a camp bed; how to build a fire, and how to be positive that it is extinguished after use; what sanitary arrangements are necessary; how to leave a clean camp site.

Canoeing Skills — If you expect to do all or much of your traveling

On a canoe trip, the Orienteering compass makes it possible for you to travel in straight lines toward river mouths or portage points.

by canoe, a lot of specialized training is necessary before you set out: You need to be a good swimmer, completely at home in the water. And you need to know how to handle a canoe: how to launch and land a canoe; what strokes to use in paddling under various conditions; how to prepare the canoe for portaging; the actual technique of portaging; how to play safe on rivers and on lakes under all possible weather conditions.

These skills can be mastered in the field only. If you are or have been a member of an outdoor club, or one of our major youth movements — the Boy Scouts or the Girl Scouts — you will probably already have had your share of hiking and camping, swimming and canoeing. Otherwise, you will have to get your training by tying in with some local group of outdoorsmen.

Certain books may be of assistance to you by suggesting methods and shortcuts. General hiking and camping skills are described in the *Scout Field Book* and the *Handbook for Boys* of the Boy Scouts of America. For more advanced camping skills, Horace Kephart's *Camping and Woodcraft* (Macmillan) is the old stand-by. For light-weight trail camping, *Going Light with Backpack or Burro* (published by the Sierra Club, San Francisco, Cal.) is particularly helpful. And if it is canoe traveling you are hankering for, you had better get hold of Carle W. Handel's *Canoe Camping* (A. S. Barnes and Co., N. Y.) and Calvin Rutstrum's *Way of the Wilderness* (Burgess Publishing Co., Minneapolis, Minn.).

Planning Your Trip

Where do you want to go? That'll be the first thing for you to decide. So study the map of the United States and Canada and select your territory. There are lots of places to pick from among National Parks and Wilderness Areas, State Parks and Provincial Parks scattered over the whole continent. For canoeing, certain states and provinces are particularly generously supplied with wilderness lakes and waterways: Maine, Minnesota, New York, Wisconsin; New Brunswick, Ontario and Quebec.

The next step is to secure topographic maps of the area you have selected for your traveling. For the regular run of topographic maps, follow the procedure described on page 10. For traveling in National Parks, drop a line to the U. S. National Parks Service, Washington 25, D.C., and ask for "Checklist of Topographic Maps of the National Parks." For trips in State Parks, write for maps to the Chamber of Commerce or Department of Conservation of the state involved. At the same time, ask for information in regard to camping and canoeing in

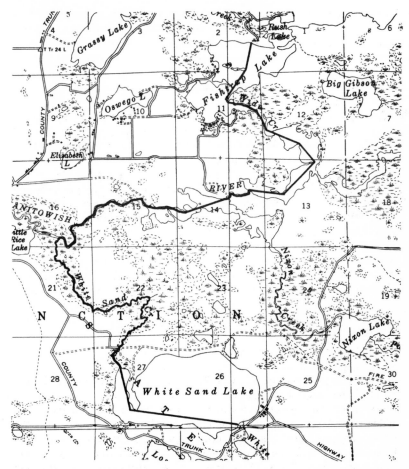

Lay out your tentative canoe route on a topographic map, then secure local information. Straight lines indicate laps traveled by compass.

the area. Many states have special literature with tips for travelers, campers, hunters and fishermen.

Laying Out Your Route

Now lay out the route you intend to follow through what you consider the most suitable area. Don't be overambitious—a daily stint of around ten miles of hiking is probably all you will care to do if you are in good condition, and around fifteen miles of canoeing. Don't plan to be on the trail every day of your expedition—schedule certain days for stopover where you may occupy yourself with your hobby of fishing or hunting or photography or nature study or whatever it happens to be—or for lazying, if that's what you want to do.

Getting Local Information

When you have decided on your route, the time has come to secure local information. In some instances, you may be able to depend on the maps alone and on printed information, but conditions often change, and you had better make certain of what you can expect before you set out: Where equipment may be bought or rented; whether food supplies may be purchased along the route or must be toted from the jumping-off place; what camp sites are available and what the regulations are for their use; whether certain streams are navigable, certain portages passable. You can generally secure this information by dropping a line (with a stamped and self-addressed return envelope) to the "Postmaster" or "General Store" of the village closest to your starting point.

Setting Out

With all preparations taken care of, you are ready to set out. And if your qualifications are as good as they ought to be for the kind of trip you have planned, you should be able to carry it through with flying colors and have the time of your life.

But there is that little "if."

If for any reason you are not completely positive about your qualifications for an expedition on your own, it will pay you to set your mind at rest by taking along a registered guide for your first trip into a new wilderness area. The next time you come back to the same area you will then have the necessary training and confidence to do the job on your own.

In any event, before setting out on a wilderness trip, provide the local forest ranger or game warden with an itinerary of your trip. Then in case anything unforeseen should happen, it will be comparatively easy for the "outside world" to reach you.

Know Where You Are

As you travel along, the most important rule is: *Know at all times*

Map Symbols for Special WATER FEATURES — Blue

Intermittent lake or pond..

Large rapids..

Small rapids...

Large falls...

Small falls..

Canal, flume, or aqueduct...

Water elevation..*870*

When planning a canoe trip, pay special attention to these map symbols. Rapids are for the trained canoeist only; falls necessitate portaging.

where you are, according to your map; and the direction in which you are going, according to your compass.

Before you set out from one point to the next, locate your position on your map. Then, take exact compass reading, compensate for declination, figure out the distance and the approximate time for arrival at your destination, take accurate bearings from landmark to landmark, and follow your route on the map itself.

Taking Cross-Bearings

In hilly or mountainous territories, ridges and tops will assist you in determining your location, provided you know how to read your map contours. But in wood-covered lake areas, spattered with a multitude of small islands, it may be difficult for you to determine exactly where you are, which island you are passing. For deciding your location in that kind of territory, you may have to resort to the trick of taking cross-bearings — or "resection," if you want to be technical.

In taking cross-bearings, you locate first two landmarks in the field which are clearly indicated on your map. Next, you take a back-bearing to each of them and compensate each bearing for magnetic declination. You then project the two back-bearings to your map, and draw the bearing lines forward from the landmarks toward your location. You are located where the two bearings cross or "resect" each other.

For a specific example of taking cross-bearings, study the map on page 121.

You want to know on which of the small islands in the lake you have landed. You can see a farm to the left and a hilltop to the right. Both of them are shown on your map. You take a back-bearing toward the farm-house by sighting *against* the direction-of-travel arrow of your orienteering compass and turning the compass housing until the compass is oriented with the north part of the needle at rest over the orienting arrow, north tip of needle pointing to N. Now you have the magnetic back-bearing. How many degrees? 154 — right!

Now place the compass on the map with one back corner touching the farmhouse. Using the farmhouse as an axis, swing the base plate of your Orienteering compass, *without changing the position of the housing in relation to the plate,* until the orienting arrow of the compass housing lies parallel to the nearest magnetic-north line of the map. Hold down the base plate firmly, and draw a line forward from the farmhouse, along the edge of the base plate.

You are located somewhere on this line. But where?

To find the exact location you take a similar back-bearing to the hill-top, place back corner of base plate on map at hilltop symbol, swing compass until orienting arrow lies parallel to magnetic-north line, and draw line along the edge of the base plate, forward from the hilltop.

You are located where this second line cuts the first.

Cross-Bearing Practice — Cross-bearings may appear rather tricky, but you will easily master the idea after a couple of tries.

WHERE ARE YOU?   INDOOR PRACTICE

PURPOSE — Practice in locating your position on the map by cross-bearings.

TEST YOURSELF — Bring out the training map and training compass from the back of the book, then find your position in each of the following cases:

1. Where are you located if you can see the top of Record Hill at a back-bearing of 240° (the direction *from* Record Hill *toward* you is 240°), and the westernmost cabin of Camp Adirondack at a back-bearing of 292° (from that cabin toward the point where you are: 292°)? . . . .

2. Where are you if Meadow Knoll Cemetery is at back-reading 46°, top of Hutton Hill as back-bearing 6°? . . . .

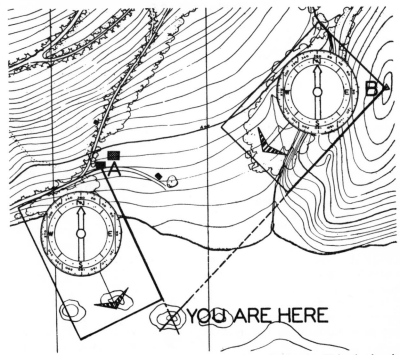

To find your location, take back-readings toward two landmarks. Using landmark symbols as axis, draw lines. You are located where lines cross.

3. Where are you if the back-bearing to Anthony's Nose is 285° and the back-bearing to Glenburnie Hotel (large building at Glenburnie) is 309°?. . . . .

4. Where are you if Log Chapel is at back-bearing 301°, westernmost point of Camp Adirondack peninsula at back-bearing 38°? . . . .

(For the answers, turn to page 132.)

AS GAME—Each player has pencil, training map, and training compass (in Orienteering Training Kit, see page 133). Leader slowly reads out the two back-bearings in each of the questions above—or in similar questions worked out by himself. First player with correct answer scores 25 points; up to 100 points for correct answers to all four questions.

A FINAL WORD

In spite of all your Orienteering skill, there may be times when you feel yourself in doubt about your location or direction. Under such conditions what can you do?

Well, there is one thing you can't do: You can't get lost with a map and a compass in your hands — not if you use your "noodle." So stop and think! Take it easy! With a bit of figuring and logical reasoning you should get yourself back on the course if you happen to be off:

First of all — did you set your compass bearing correctly from your map? Did you compensate for declination by using a map provided with Magnetic-North lines that automatically take care of the declination? Or did you use the method of resetting the compass repeatedly for the declination? In the first case, your destination will probably be still ahead of you — your progress was slower than you expected. In the latter case, you may have slipped up on the resetting, and your destination may be waiting for you somewhere to one side of you — to the right of you in areas of westerly declination, to the left where the declination is easterly.

If you still find yourself stymied, you may decide to return to your starting point by following the back-reading of your compass — by traveling backward against the direction-of-travel arrowhead instead of with it, as described on page 63. Even better, if there is a long, "catching" landmark ahead of you — a road, a railroad, a river, a lakeshore — you can aim for that and then reschedule your trip from the spot you hit.

Best of all — evade any possibility of going wrong by following to the letter the practices of correct Orienteering: By planning your trip carefully before starting out, by setting your compass correctly, by compensating for declination, by studying your map repeatedly, by following your compass and trusting it to get you to your destination.

"Practice makes master," they say. *Orienteering Practice Makes the Master Orienteerer.* The more practice you get, the more certain you become and the less apt you are ever to be in doubt of your location on your trips.

So make it a habit always to bring along compass and map — even on short trips — and take every chance to practice and to experience

The Sport of "ORIENTEERING"

APPENDIX

MAP MAKING WITH THE ORIENTEERING COMPASS

From time to time you may have occasion to make a sketch map of an area for your own use or for the sake of informing others of "the lay of the land." It is an easy matter to produce such a map with the help of an Orienteering compass. The Orienteering compass combines all the instruments needed for simple surveying: a compass for determining directions, a protractor for laying out angles, a ruler for drawing direction lines, an inch-rule (on some models also a centimeter-rule) for measuring distances.

In addition to the compass you will need a pencil and a sheet of fairly heavy drawing paper attached to a firm backing (plywood or thick cardboard). Or use a drawing pad, about 9 by 12 inches.

Before taking off on your mapping expedition, draw parallel lines, 1 inch apart, across your paper. These lines are similar to the magnetic-north lines you drew across your map to compensate for compass declination. Write the word "North" along the top edge of your paper to make certain that your directions are always properly oriented.

Making the Traverse

Out in the field you need to decide on a suitable spot on your paper for starting your map. If your area lies along a straight route – known as an "open traverse" – you will want to start close to one side of your paper. If the area lies within a more or less circular route that ends where it starts – a "closed traverse" – you need to give more consideration to the place of starting. If the area lies to the north of you, you will start the traverse near the bottom edge of the paper, half way from either side. If it lies to the northwest of you, you will start the traverse near the lower right hand corner of your paper. Indicate the starting point with an "X" and get going.

Determining Directions

For the first lap of your traverse, face in the direction you plan to go, toward the point where the route makes its first turning and set the compass for the first bearing in the usual way (as described in detail on page 60): Hold the Orienteering compass level before you, with the direction-of-travel arrowhead pointing straight ahead of you. Twist the compass housing until the compass needle lies over the orienting arrow on the bottom of the housing, with its north part pointing to the letter N on the top of the housing. Don't bother to read the degrees and don't note down any degree number—this chore is eliminated when you use an Orienteering compass.

Transfer the direction to the paper by placing the compass on the paper with the edge of the base plate touching the "X" (your starting location) and with the direction-of-travel arrowhead pointing in the direction you are going. Disregarding the compass needle, turn the compass, without disturbing the setting, until the orienting arrow on the bottom of the housing lies parallel to the magnetic-north lines, with the arrowpoint to the North. Holding the compass firmly on the paper, draw a line along the edge of the base plate.

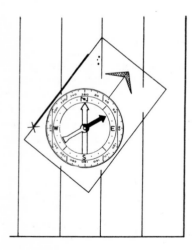
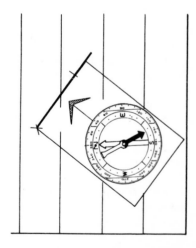

Set compass for lap of traverse. Make "X" mark on paper for starting point. Place compass, draw direction.

Walk off distance of first lap. Place inch-rule of base plate along direction line. Mark off distance.

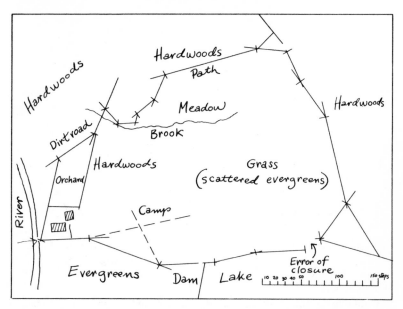

This is how a completed "closed traverse" looks. Note how location of "Camp" was determined by triangulation. Note also "error of closure." (⅓ size.)

Measuring Distances

Next walk the distance to the turn in the road while counting your steps and mark off the distance on the map at the scale you have decided to use.

A scale of ¼ inch for each 10 steps (about 25 feet) will give you a map in a scale of approximately 1 inch to 100 feet — or, in map language, 1:1200. Your 9-by-12-inch sheet will accommodate an open traverse 1,100 feet long or a closed traverse about 4,000 feet in circumference.

Another suitable scale is ⅛ inch for each 10 steps (about 25 feet). This will give you a map in a scale of around 1 inch to 200 feet — or, in map language, 1:2400. At this scale you can manage to get an open traverse 2,200 feet long or a closed traverse 8,000 feet in circumference onto your sheet.

For argument's sake, let's say that you decide on the 1:1200 scale of ¼ inch = 10 steps. Let's also say that the first distance you measure

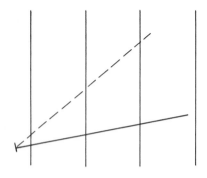

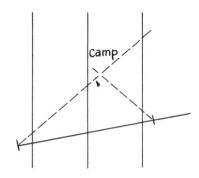

To determine position of distant object by triangulation, take bearing to object and of road ahead.

At next point, take another bearing to object. Draw bearings on map. Object lies where bearings cross.

amounts to 60 steps. In that case, 60 steps in the field become 6 x ¼ inch = 1½ inch on your map. Using the inch-rule along one edge of the base plate of your Orienteering compass, you mark off this distance along the first direction line.

Continue in this fashion taking bearings and stepping off distances and putting bearings and distances on the map, until you have completed your traverse.

Including the Details

As you cover each of the laps, make notes of the features you want to include on your finished map—such as vegetation features (hardwood trees, evergreens, grassland, meadow), man-made features (buildings, bridges), and water features (brooks, rivers, lakes).

Instead of stepping off the distances to objects far off the road on either side, you can determine their positions by triangulation: At the first station where you see the object, take a bearing on the object as well as of the road ahead and include both bearings on the map. At your next station, take another bearing toward the object and mark this on your map. The object is located where the bearings cross (see illustration above).

Error of Closure

Your complete traverse will have the general appearance of the sketch on page 125. You will notice that start and finish do not co-

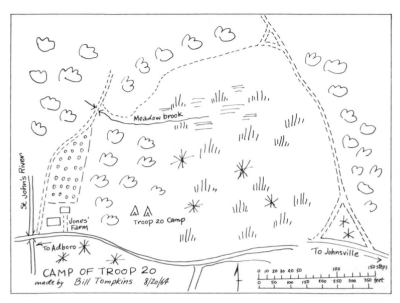

Finished map sketch should contain magnetic-north half-arrow, scale of steps and of feet, name of area, name of map maker, date, designations. (⅓ size.)

incide. Such a gap—known as "error of closure"—cannot be overcome, even by the best surveyor. It is perfectly all right as long as it is not excessive. If it is, it is obvious that you have made a mistake along the way and need to re-walk part of your traverse.

Finishing the Map

The final map you can draw at home. Here you can do a neat job of inking in all the landscape features, using enlarged versions of regular map symbols (pages 16-21) to fit the scale of your map.

Wind up your map-making by including on your map a magnetic-north half-arrow (along one of the magnetic-north lines already on the map), a scale showing the number of your steps and another giving the scale in feet (as determined in the way described on page 42), the name of the area, the name of the map maker, the date, and whatever specific designations may be necessary, such as the name of the river, the name of the owner of the farm, and so on.

GLOSSARY

BACK-BEARING—the direction or bearing *from* a visible landmark *to* your location (page 121). Used in taking CROSS-BEARINGS (see below).

BACK-READING—looking back over the compass toward the point from which you came (page 74).

BASE PLATE—the rectangular plate of the Orienteering compass on which the compass housing is mounted (page 59).

BEARING—Originally the nautical term for: the direction of an object from the ship. In Orienteering defined as "a direction stated in compass degrees" (page 60).

CARDINAL POINTS—the four principal points of the compass: north, east, south, and west (page 58).

COMPASS—instrument for determining directions with the help of a strip of magnetized steel swinging on a pivot (page 51).

COMPASS, CONVENTIONAL—a compass generally enclosed in a watch-case-type of housing (page 56).

COMPASS, ORIENTEERING—see ORIENTEERING COMPASS.

CONTOUR INTERVAL—the distance in height between one contour line and the one next to it (page 20).

CONTOUR LINE—an imaginary line in the field along which every point is at the same height above sea level (page 19).

CROSS-BEARINGS—two or more bearings which, when transferred to a map, indicate your location at the point at which they cross (page 78 and 121).

CULTURAL FEATURES—man-made landscape features: roads, buildings, etc. (page 15).

DECLINATION—the angle between the direction toward which the compass needle points and the true north line; the difference in degrees between magnetic north direction and true north direction in any given locality (page 90).

DIAL, COMPASS—the rim or edge of the compass housing, usually marked with the initials of the cardinal points and graduated in the 360 degrees of a circle (page 59).

DIRECTION—the relative location of one landscape feature from another (page 25). See also BEARING.

DIRECTION-OF-TRAVEL ARROWHEAD—the arrowhead on the base plate of the Orienteering compass which points in the direction of travel when the compass is oriented (page 59).

HOUSING—the part of the compass which "houses" the needle; some times turnable, on some compasses liquid-filled (page 59).

HYDROGRAPHIC FEATURES—water features: streams, lakes, etc. From Greek *hydro* water, and *graphein,* to write (pages 15, 18 and 121).

HYPSOGRAPHIC FEATURES—elevations: hills and valleys. From Greek *hypso* height, and *graphein,* to write (pages 15 and 19).

INDEX POINTER—the line on the base plate of the Orienteering compass against which the degree number of the dial on the compass housing is read (page 59).

INTERCARDINAL POINTS—the four points of the compass between the four CARDINAL POINTS: north-east, south-east, south-west, north-west.

LANDMARK—a feature in the landscape which can be readily recognized—anything from a prominent tree or rock, to a church or a lake.

LATITUDE—imaginary lines on the globe running parallel to the Equator; distance in degrees north and south from Equator (page 14).

LONGITUDE—imaginary lines on the globe running from pole to pole; distance in degrees east and west from Greenwich, England (page 13).

MAP—a reduced representation of a portion of the surface of the earth (page 6).

MAP SYMBOLS—small designs used on a map to indicate the features of a landscape (page 15).

MERIDIAN LINES—lines on the map or imaginary lines in the field running true north to true south (page 13).

ORIENTATION—the process of determining one's location in the field with the help of landscape features, map, or compass, or with all three combined.

ORIENTEERING—the skill or the process of finding your way in the field with map and compass combined. A coined word and trademark registered by American Orienteering Service to identify an outdoor program based on the use of map and compass, as well as to identify certain services rendered and products distributed by A. O. S. for this sport.

ORIENTEERING COMPASS—a compass especially designed to simplify the process of finding your way with map and compass. Usually has its compass housing mounted on a rectangular base plate in such a way that it can be turned easily (page 58).

ORIENTING ARROW—arrow-marking or parallel lines in or on housing of Orienteering compass; used for setting the compass (page 59).

ORIENTING, COMPASS—holding compass in such a way that the directions of its dial coincide with the same directions in the field. Done by turning the whole compass, with the dial set at a degree number (page 62), or by twisting the compass housing with the direction-of-travel arrowhead pointing toward a landmark (page 60), until the compass needle coincides with and is parallel with the orienting arrow of the compass housing.

ORIENTING, MAP—turning map in such a way that what is north on the map corresponds with north in the field. Done by "inspection" (page 41), or with the help of a compass (page 95).

PACE—double step (page 42).

PROTRACTOR—instrument used for measuring angles, usually in terms of degrees (page 28).

QUADRANGLE—a rectangular tract of land depicted on a map (page 10).

RESECTION—determining a location by cross-bearings (page 119).

SCALE—the proportion between a distance on the map and the actual distance in the field (page 6).

SILVA—trademark registered by Silva Industries Inc. Used to identify Orienteering compasses and other types of high grade compasses.

TOPOGRAPHIC MAPS—maps of high precision. From the Greek *topos* place, and *graphein* to write (page 6).

VARIATION—another term for DECLINATION.

ANSWERS TO TESTS

MAP SYMBOL QUIZ (pages 22-23)

1. Road (improved dirt)
2. Contour lines (hill)
3. Cemeteries
4. Railroad (single track)
5. Spring
6. Well
7. Buildings
8. Bench mark (monumented)
9. Marsh
10. Trail
11. Bridge (river, road)
12. Triangulation station
13. River (streams)
14. Road (unimproved dirt)
15. Sand dunes
16. Church
17. School

CONTOUR QUIZ (pages 24-25)

1. (a) almost level
2. (a) from bottom of map
   to top of map
3. (b) a slow grade, rising
   only 40 feet
4. (a) a slow-moving stream
5. (a) Hutton Hill
   (c) Niger Marsh
   (e) Huckleberry Mountain

TAKE POINT BEARINGS (pages 30-31)

1. 73°	2. 297°	3. 50°	4. 274°	5. 160°
6. 168°	7. 126°	8. 183°	9. 160°	10. 346°

(Bearings are figured from the center of one landmark to the center of the other. Permissible error: Two degrees more or less)

DIRECTION QUIZ (page 34)

1. 358°   2. 97°   3. 252°   4. 80°   5. 106°

(Bearings are figured from the center of one landmark to the center of the other. Permissible error: Two degrees more or less)

DISTANCE QUIZ (pages 36-37)

1. 7,100 feet   2. 2,900 feet   3, 21,400 feet
4. 4,000   5. 12,200

(Distances are figured from the center of one landmark to the center of the other. Permissible error: 100 feet more or less)

Find Places on the Map (pages 38-39)

1. Glenburnie
2. Crossroads (x455)
3. Crossroads (432)
4. Church (cemetery)
5. Crossroads (432)
6. Hill 384
7. Road-T (441)
8. Road-Bend
9. Crossroads (455)
10. Start of stream

Compass Competition (pages 69-70)

Start Point 1:
  Destination Point 7
Start Point 3:
  Destination Point 2
Start Point 5:
  Destination Point 16
Start Point 7:
  Destination Point 8
Start Point 9:
  Destination Point 15

Start Point 2:
  Destination Point 19
Start Point 4:
  Destination Point 8
Start Point 6:
  Destination Point 8
Start Point 8:
  Destination Point 9
Start Point 10:
  Destination Point 19

Compass Setting Quiz (pages 86-87)

1. 94°   2. 4°   3. 292°   4. 262°   5. 224°

(Bearings are figured from the center of one landmark to the center of the other. Permissible error: Two degrees more or less)

What Do You Find? (page 88)

1. Church
2. Road-T, Glenburnie
3. Top of Record Hill
4. Road-T (381)
5. Marsh

Where Are You? (pages 120-121)

1. Friends Point
2. South tip of Niger Marsh
3. Indian Kettles
4. Record Hill

VALUABLE ADDRESSES

For information on Competitive Orienteering Racing in the U.S.A. write to

U.S. Orienteering Federation, Suite 317, 933 North Kenmore Street, Arlington, Virginia 22201.

(In Canada: The Canadian Orienteering Federation, P.O.B. #6206, Terminal A, Toronto 1, Canada)

For information on Teaching and Training Aids (like practicing compasses and protractors, training maps, compass training demonstrators, etc.) and on other textbooks, write to

American Orienteering Service, P.O.B. #547, La Porte, Indiana 46350.

(In Canada: Canadian Orienteering Service, 446 McNicolls Avenue, Willowdale, Ont. Canada)

For information about films on map-and-compass use and on Orienteering, write to

The International Film Bureau, 332 South Michigan Avenue, Chicago, Illinois 60604.

(In Canada: Educational Film Distributors Ltd., 191 Eglinton Avenue East, Toronto 12, Canada)

SPECIAL ORIENTEERING MAPS

To make Orienteering racing still more fun, special Orienteering maps have been developed under the guidance of The International Orienteering Federation. These maps are much more detailed and precise than regular topographic maps and are produced in a larger scale (1:10,000 – 1:25,000). So far the availability in North America is limited, but there are such maps for the Ward Pound Ridge Reservation, Westchester County, New York, for areas close to the U.S. Marine Corps, Quantico, Virginia, for the Southern Illinois University, Carbondale, Illinois, and for some areas of the Philmont Scout Ranch & Explorer Base, Cimarron, New Mexico. In Canada several areas in the Provinces of Quebec and Ontario have been mapped this way. For up-to-date information contact the appropriate Orienteering Federations at the addresses stated above.

"Orienteering" ®

COMPASSES

Ask your dealer to demonstrate the different SILVA models or write for complete information by using the convenient post card in the envelope on the inside back cover of this book.

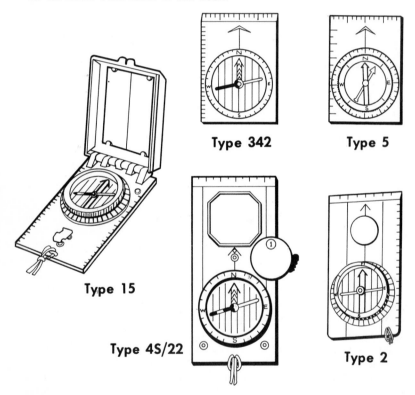

Type 342

Type 5

Type 15

Type 4S/22

Type 2

Orienteering ® films available are: BY MAP AND COMPASS, ORIEN-TEERING ® , and THE INVISIBLE FORCE OF DIRECTION. All films are for sale or rental, and in some cases, free of charge. For information write to: INTERNATIONAL FILM BUREAU, INC., 332 South Michigan Avenue, Chicago, Illinois 60604.

INDEX